The day Vonnie and I met Brooke Stevens, we knew she was an extraordinary person. In her book, *Building on a Christ-Centered Foundation: A Study of Faith, Hope, and Love* she teaches that in spite of varied life position and experience, we all need the common life foundation of Jesus. She carefully articulates that by walking in His footsteps, through the power of the Holy Spirit, believers can confidently face the challenges of building the Christian life. Her personal experiences, weaved with scripture and story combine in a beautiful recipe for the making of a blessed life for the Christ follower.

—Woody Wright, Singer, Songwriter, Publisher, Would He Write Songs

Building on a Christ-Centered Foundation: A Study of Faith, Hope, and Love is a powerful and relatable guide for anyone navigating their walk with Christ. With vivid imagery and heartfelt reflections, Stevens challenges readers to examine their own spiritual journey and take bold steps toward a deeper relationship with God. I highly recommend this book for its inspiring message and practical encouragement to live out your faith daily.

—Robyn Dykstra, International Christian Speaker and Author

In *Building on a Christ-Centered Foundation: A Study of Faith, Hope, and Love* we are told how we can experience the "abundant" life that God desires us to have. This book is a wonderful read about the eternal qualities that God has "gifted" us with to help us on our journey of life. The real-life stories and examples have a way of capturing one's attention, encouraging and challenging us to build our lives on the "Christ-Centered Foundation." Brooke's love and passion for God is "contagious"! I enthusiastically recommend this book to those who are wanting to deepen their relationship with God and grow, deeper, spiritually.

—Rev. Dr Jim "Umfundisi" Lo, Director of World Missions, Churches of God (Holiness), Emeritus Professor of Practical Theology and Intercultural Studies, Indiana Wesleyan University

I love to hear the stories of God's children. I know you will be inspired and deeply touched by Booke's story as I have been. She has beautifully gathered her reflections and encouragement around love, faith, and hope—three powerful words that have guided her life's story.

—Henry Smith, Ph.D. President Emeritus,
Indiana Wesleyan University

A strong foundation begins with a single brick, and Brooke Stevens shows readers how to lay each one with purpose. Through timeless biblical truths, relatable personal stories, and thought-provoking review questions, she equips believers with the tools needed to build a life of faith that can weather any storm.

—Tracy DeGraaf, Comedian and Author of *Laugh Anyway, Mom*

Brooke Stevens paints vivid pictures that stick in the reader's minds while helping them navigate an often-tumultuous life. She makes it clear that we start with Jesus as our foundation but adds how important it is to stand on the three building blocks; faith, hope, and love. While these tools work together in guiding us on this journey, Stevens creates clear scenarios and illustrations that make it come to life. In her book, she writes, "Faith anchors us to God, hope will keep us heavenly-minded, love is how we react to everyone we encounter and to the Lord, himself." Once you begin navigating through the pages, this book will become like a companion on your faith journey.

—Burchfield Brothers, Concert Artists

Are you unsure what being a Christian looks like? Do you want your faith to have a strong foundation? Then you will want to read *Building on a Christ-Centered Foundation*. Brooke packed *Building on a Christ-Centered Foundation* full of scripture, Biblical wisdom, and personal stories that will guide you to a strong relationship with God.

—Beth Gormong, Coauthor of *Growing the Fruit of the Spirit, Hello, Beautiful!* and *Yes, You Can!*

Brooke Stevens takes us on a journey to learn the ways of discipleship and faithfulness. Drawn from the personal adventures of her own faith journey and the mentoring she received from others, Brooke shows us the fruitful path to a Spirit led life. Brooke's stories and rich illustrations make the portrait of the disciple's journey come to life. This is recommended reading for all who seek to develop the characteristics and disciplines of a victorious Christian life.

—Rev Wayne Richards, CEO of Habitat For Missions

Building on a Christ-Centered Foundation takes readers on an inspiring spiritual journey toward a life overflowing with faith, hope, and love. Filled with engaging stories, powerful metaphors, and rich biblical insights, this book is a testament to the meaningful message God has given Brooke Stevens to share. No matter where you are in your spiritual journey, you will find wisdom and encouragement within these pages.

—Dr. Mark O. Wilson, Associate Professor of Christian Ministry, Southern Wesleyan University

Building
on a
Christ-Centered Foundation

STUDY *of* FAITH, HOPE, *and* LOVE

BROOKE STEVENS

EABooks Publishing
Your Partner In Publishing

ISBN: 978-1-966382-24-9

Cover design: Robin Black
Cover photo: Pexels

Published by EABooks Publishing, a division of
Living Parables of Central Florida, Inc. a 501c3
EABooksPublishing.com

Table of Contents

Dedication

First and foremost, this book is dedicated to the Lord. Thank you for saving my life and changing its course. Thank you for never giving up on me and giving me a second chance at life. Thank you for calling me to share about you with others. I can never thank you enough for your many blessings and for being my friend.

And to my family who have faithfully supported and encouraged me throughout this journey:

Dad and Mom (Kevin and Ronda), thank you for starting me on my journey of faith, introducing me to Jesus and supporting me along the way.

My brother, Drew, and his wife, Charly, and their boys, Oakley and Koa, I am so proud of you and thankful for each one of you. It has been a blessing to see your family continuing to grow and watch you raise the next generation of our family on the foundation of Jesus.

My sister, Rachel (Karilyn), and her husband, Camden, I am so proud of you both and your journeys for Jesus. You both are faithfully serving the Lord, and I can hardly wait to see what he does next in your lives. Rachel, thank you for being one of my closest friends, biggest encouragers, and helping me grow in my faith. Thanks for always believing in me.

Papaw and Memaw (Dave and Mary Lou), I have been blessed to not only know my grandparents but to also call them some of my closest friends. Thank you for being there for me every step of the way and praying for me every day of my life. Thank you for building our family on Jesus and helping point us to him when we lost our way.

My uncle Tony who has been a part of my life since I was a child and supported us all. You have impacted countless people for Jesus, and I am thankful for you.

To my Nebraska family, though farther away, but still close to my heart, Grandpa Ron; Grandpa Lyle; Grandma Karen; Uncle Tony and his daughter, Chelzie; Aunt Tonya and Uncle Matt, and their kids, Caleb, Leah, and Canaan.

To Steven, my love and my friend. Thank you for all of your support and encouragement along this journey. And to Pete, Ronda, Laura, and Rachel, I have been blessed by your friendship. Thanks for cheering me on.

To my friends and mentors, Phil and Rhonda, Bub and Brenda, Larry and Sandra, and countless others, who if I listed them all, the list would be as long as this book. I am so thankful for all of you and the impact you have made on my life. You all have taught me so much about growing in the Lord and helped me grow in my relationship with Christ.

And to my Forever friend on the other side of the world who believed in me and knew I would become an author years before I even dreamed about writing this book.

Faith, Hope, and Love: The Building Blocks

Along the mountainside, an ancient wall flowed and ebbed up and down across the terrain. As we drove along, the artifact continued with us. Eventually the tour bus stopped and our group ventured towards the massive structure called the Great Wall of China. We started at the base of the structure where a staircase led into another until we reached a slight platform with two massive staircases heading in opposite directions.

As we began the epic trek, we quickly noticed the variety in the steps as we climbed and descended the mountainside. Some of the stairs were steep and required great effort to climb. Other parts of the path were flat terrain with rounded boards for footing that stretched across the walkway. These areas also held more modern-sized stair steps. Each step was unique, so as beautiful as the mountaintop views were, it was more important to watch the steps as we climbed so that we would not stumble and fall.

Just like we needed to start at the ground at the base of the Great Wall, we all start somewhere in life. Some of us started in a loving home; others started in a broken home. Some were born in a prosperous country;

others were born in poor countries. Some of us have full function of our extremities; others started with a physical handicap. No matter where we start, we start somewhere.

When we become Christians, we start somewhere in the journey of life. Some of us accepted Jesus at a young age, while others took the leap of faith much later in life. No matter where we start, we start with Jesus as our foundation.

On top of this foundation, the Lord gives us building blocks to stand on. These become the steps of our journey of faith. Some of the steps are massive, and it's hard to picture how to even begin to climb atop them. Then another step feels much more manageable and our confidence begins to grow. The size of each person's step will vary, just as the size of each of the steps fluctuated at the Great Wall. Three sturdy building blocks or first steps on our staircase are faith, hope, and love. By using these three Christian attributes as first steps on our staircases, they will strengthen the believer's foundation so when the next steps are added the staircase continues to get stronger.

We are first going to look at where the Bible refers to faith, hope, and love together and how they relate to each other. First Corinthians 13:13 (ESV) reads, "So now faith, hope and love abide, these three; but the greatest of these is love."

Faith, hope, and love are three key principles for helping believers navigate godly lives. They are eternal qualities, withstanding the weathering of life's journey. Faith, hope, and love are Christ-like qualities that the Holy Spirit uses to guide believers along the way. Once someone has accepted Christ, the pattern of his or her life will take one of two directions. Either the person will grow in the love and wisdom of Christ or the person will become stagnant and lukewarm, which leads to falling away from the faith. Revelation 3:15–16 (ESV) reads, "I know your deeds, that you are neither cold nor hot. I wish you were either one or the other! So, because you are lukewarm—neither hot nor cold—I am about to spit you out of my mouth."

In the above scripture, being cold describes a person walking far from God, while being hot is to be a Christian who is passionately pursuing God. Lukewarm living is like drifting along with the current on top of a log that's heading downstream. You are not swimming, you are not drowning, but at some point, there is a waterfall ahead. If you are drowning, you can call out for help, and the Savior steps in to pull you out. If you are swimming, you can help lead others to shore and out of harm's way.

However, on top of the log, you coast along blissfully unaware of others either swimming or drowning in the water. Each day begins looking like the previous one until the day that gentle river drops 100 feet from underneath you. But if you are on the log, take heart, for the Savior is ready to hold your hand and help you jump off that log if you will call out to Him. He can turn any situation around. He is able, and he is good.

First and foremost, we need to pray and read scripture in order to grow in Christ. We also need encouragement from a strong support system. By this, I mean we need other Christians who are on the same path as we are on. We can often find this support for developing our faith in a strong church environment. In a church, we encounter servant-hearted leaders, mentors, pastors, teachers, worship leaders, greeters, and children's workers. Besides those in specific leadership roles, all of those in the congregation are part of the church body and can help us develop our faith.

For example, my dad is a wonderful driver. He has driven to family events from Indiana to Nebraska and Illinois to Ohio and everywhere in between. When I was growing up and my dad was driving in bad weather, he would tell me, "Remember to get your wingman." What is a wingman? "That is a pilot's term referring to when the aircraft is positioned behind and outside the leading aircraft in a formation." [i]

My dad would find a vehicle heading in the same direction and traveling at a similar speed, and he would follow just enough behind that he could watch the other car. If rain were falling, the car ahead would avoid puddles. If snow were falling, there would be a fresh path that created better traction. If fog blanketed the air, the lead car's taillights would point the way.

This reminds me of what it's like to be a part of the church body.

You find people who believe in Jesus and they have been in similar circumstances or are just a few steps ahead. In the rainstorms of life, they show you the puddles to either avoid or slow down to cross over. In snow, or places where the path is hard to find, they clear a path so you can see God is the smooth way through. And in fog, they shine a light to illuminate the Word of God so you know how to head in the right direction. Sometimes we are the ones following, and at other times, we are the lead car for someone else.

These people are often referred to as spiritual mentors and their mentees. First Corinthians 3:10–15 (ESV) expands this concept further by showing that how one person builds up another is critical to their success, "According to the grace of God given to me, like a skilled master builder I laid a foundation, and someone else is building upon it. Let each one take care how he builds upon it. For no one can lay a foundation other than that which is laid, which is Jesus Christ. Now if anyone builds on the foundation with gold, silver, precious stones, wood, hay, straw—each one's work will become manifest, for the Day will disclose it, because it will be revealed by fire, and the fire will test what sort of work each one has done. If the work that anyone has built on the foundation survives, he will receive a reward. If anyone's work is burned up, he will suffer loss, though he himself will be saved, but only as through fire."

The church is vital to build up one another; the church consists of the people of God not merely the building where they worship. First Corinthians 3:16 (ESV) explains it this way, "Do you not know that you are God's temple and that God's Spirit dwells in you?" If we house the Holy Spirit in our hearts, then we are the church.

My experience with the church started at a young age. I accepted Jesus when I was a child, but my life was not always in line after that. After several rebellious years, I rededicated my life to Jesus when I was 19 years old. Because I had been raised in a church, I knew a lot of the Bible stories, but what I needed to do was to plant my feet on the foundation I had accepted as a child: Jesus Christ.

The first few years after we accept Jesus are a vital time for growing in faith. I want to encourage every believer to find a strong Christian environment where they can grow. To do this, find a church founded on the Bible.

During my teenage years, I found out firsthand that it is not possible to be a stagnant Christian. Like in the illustration of the log, we are either growing and swimming in the right direction, or we are sinking beneath the waves.

We need to anchor ourselves in Jesus and build on our foundation on him as the rock beneath our feet. In doing so, we can weather any storm. God is greater than any trial we may face. Often, we go into a situation empty handed, but we do not have to be unarmed if we choose to go through the situation with Christ.

Faith, hope, and love are tools we learn to use to build this foundation on Christ. Being connected to other mature believers can help teach us about building a strong foundation on Jesus.

I found a group of strong Christians when I was searching for a job a few months after rededicating my life to Christ. I was walking up and down our city's main street and applying at every business along the way. I reached somewhere between fifteen and twenty establishments with no success. Then I visited my grandparents and applied for a job at a few more businesses in the city where they lived, all with no avail.

Discouraged, I rode with my grandparents to visit the Christian campground where I had attended services with them when I was little. By the grace of God, the directors were searching for summer help and offered my brother and me summer jobs. I was weak in my faith, but they taught me Biblical principles I could stand on, and at the end of that summer, they baptized me.

Being in a strong Christian environment helped me grow in loving others. I learned how to love others with godly love instead the world's version of love. The leaders at the camp showed me what faith built on the foundation of Christ looks like and how it stands the test of time. When one of my closest camp friends was passing away, I saw how hope in the promise that is to come gives us life for the day to day. Faith, hope, and love are fundamental for growth for the maturing believer.

Have you ever faced a hard trial? Did you reach the other side of it victoriously? Not victorious as the world sees victory with the old standby life motto of "Faking it till you make it," as I had often thought when it came to the trials I had faced. Instead, I mean "victorious" as in making it through the trial with God.

When we make sinful choices, our decisions will often catch back up to us with negative repercussions. But when you have been set free from sin, you are truly free! Walk in victory with Jesus!

God revealed to me that the burden of trying to figure out why I was in a specific situation was not a directive from him. The situation was there—and I had the choice to either grow through it in victory or perhaps have to repeat the same lesson later because of my own choices leading me back into it.

Throughout the Bible God tells us not to be afraid. When something comes up in my life, fear tends to be one of the first things that I feel. I have to remind myself that victory comes from giving the situation over to God. If I do not ask God to help me, I can spiral in fear and get stuck. This is a lesson that I have repeated often in my life. God tells me I do not have to be afraid and he will help me through it, I just need to remember to ask him for help.

Victory looks like peace in the storm and calm when the world is chaotic. You can't "fake it" about the peace you have. Victory is being unshaken when the wind and the waves do their best to shake us up.

There is only one path in victory and that is walking through all the storms with God. "To the one who is victorious, I will give the right to sit with me on my throne, just as I was victorious and sat down with my Father on his throne" (Revelation 3:21, ESV).

God knows what we need. He also knows how much we can handle. The burden will be too great for us to carry alone. We need to hand over our burdens, our worries, and our cares to God.

Friends, we need abide in the words of God, for they give us life. We are to live with them guiding us daily. Everyone faces trials, yet thriving in the face of a trail looks differently than merely surviving.

On hard days, I feel like all I am doing is surviving. These hard times may come through the passing of a loved one, a difficult work situation, or even getting caught up in the mundane day-to-day routines. But I am reminded that Jesus gives us life and life abundantly. He takes our surviving and transforms it into thriving.

In thriving, we push back against the schemes of the devil trying to undermine us. His entire goal for all eternity is to keep us from God because God loves us. In thriving, we walk through the trial holding God's hand for support. "For I, the Lord your God, hold your right hand; it is I who say to you, 'Fear not, I am the one who helps you'" (Isaiah 41:13, ESV).

No matter where you are in your walk of faith, God knows exactly what you need for the next stage of life. In school, you do not start with college first. You start in grade school or a similar, age-appropriate schooling. If you start with college first, you would not understand anything. Similarly, we all start as new believers and grow over time. God will guide you into a mature believer as you go along.

When I rededicated my life to Jesus, I felt like everyone else was better than I was. But I was confusing feelings with truth. You see, after we accept Christ, we are all on the journey of faith. We should not expect our beginning stages to be the same as other believers' mature stages. The Christians I met when I was a young believer were more mature, and they always seemed to know the right things to say. When I would be anxious over a decision, they reminded me to trust in the Lord and that he would make my paths straight.

When we are surrounded by more mature Christians, we see some of the strongest visuals of the Bible being lived out. They help us grow and point us back to the Word so someday soon, we can begin to point other growing believers to Jesus when they, too, face hard situations.

One of my favorite things to do is to volunteer at the Christian campground I attended as a child; the same place where I was baptized and worked that summer many years ago. Here, I get to witness firsthand the ever-growing "Walk of Faith" brick walkway. This is a path leading from the camp's tabernacle to its gazebo. The path is made of bricks with the names of believers engraved on them. Every name is someone past or present who has walked their walk of faith with Jesus, and most have passed through the campgrounds.

I often like to walk down the path and reminisce about beloved friends and family who have walked victoriously with Jesus through the trials of their life and gone home to Heaven. Their lives have touched mine and continue to reach out to other generations coming along behind them. Pastor Mike expands a famous Ram Dass' quote on his blog "A Heart for God Ministries" by saying, "As believers we are all walking each other home."[ii]

So, take my outstretched hand, and let's take a walk. One of the best lessons the Lord showed me was that faith, hope, and love are necessary to keep our feet firmly planted on the Word.

In short, faith anchors us to God. We have seen him prove time and time again that he is trustworthy and truly has great plans for us. Hope will keep us heavenly minded. We need to know where we are going and not become stagnant on our journey to get there. Love is how we react to all people we encounter and the Lord. Love demonstrates that we have Christ in us, much like a lamp glows in the darkness.

Why is love called the greatest of the three? Love is the starting place. Without love, the other two, faith and hope, have no ground to change our attitude. Love is a growing and deepening relationship with God and his people. People in pain are all around us—sad, depressed, lonely, grieving, homeless people. We can help break these labels written over their lives. First Corinthians 13:1-3 (ESV) states, "If I speak in the tongues of men and of angels, but have not love, I am a noisy gong or a clanging cymbal. And if I have prophetic powers, and understand all mysteries and all knowledge, and if I have all faith, so as to remove mountains, but have not love, I am nothing. If I give away all I have, and if I deliver up my body to be burned, but have not love, I gain nothing."

A cup of water shared in pride instead of love is a slap in the face for the receiver. We live in a world of social media. Sometimes social media can be used for good, while other times it can be used in a prideful way to elevate oneself. We should to show others love because we want to love them, instead of showing someone love because it looks good on social media. Who actually longs to look into a camera to thank another human for their kindness? There is not one that I am aware of who enjoys that treatment. Matthew 6:3–4 (ESV) says, "But when you give to the needy, do not let your left hand know what your right hand is doing, so that your giving may be in secret. And your Father who sees in secret will reward you." Let it be between you, God and the receiver.

Then faith says: God can do anything, and if what God does in my situation is what I want or not, I will still trust him. However, if we look at faith by itself without having love for God or knowing his love for us, faith looks more like this: God can do anything and he does not care about how it impacts me.

This is why it is important to stabilize ourselves in love first and foremost. With love, hope says: I have eternity in Heaven because I have accepted Jesus, and I am continuing to walk in relationship with Him, and so my hope is in that promise that Heaven is far better than anything I have ever seen on earth.

Without understanding how much God loves us, it is not even possible for us to have hope. John 3:16–18 (ESV) reminds us, "'For God so loved the world, that he gave his only Son, that whoever believes in him should not perish but have eternal life. For God did not send his Son into the world to condemn the world, but in order that the world might be saved through him. Whoever believes in him is not condemned, but whoever does not believe is condemned already, because he has not believed in the name of the only Son of God.'"

Another scripture that refers to faith, hope, and love is 1 Thessalonians 1:2–3 (ESV), which reads, "We give thanks to God always for all of you, constantly mentioning you in our prayers, remembering before our God and Father your work of faith and labor of love and steadfastness of hope in our Lord Jesus Christ."

Notice the descriptions beside each word: work of faith, labor of love, and steadfastness of hope.

Faith takes work. Our faith is developed as we get to know God by studying the scriptures and talking to him in prayer. How can we believe in someone we do not personally know? This is why we need get to know God in the ways he has readily provided to us.

A friend of mine once told me about a Sunday school session her teacher gave. The teacher said that we would learn lessons in life. We can learn them from the hand of God or the hand of Satan. If we choose the easier way by learning the lessons from God's Word we will avoid a lot of heartache and mistakes. If we choose not to heed His Word and subsequently do the things we should not do, we will still learn the lesson, but from mistakes and heartache. We will still learn the lessons of life either way, but we will not make the mistakes that cause us to learn by the hard way if we choose to learn from God's Word instead.

He teaches us these lessons from situations we face, and we can either learn from the situations or repeat the lesson again later. We choose whether or not we get to learn the lesson a second, third, or fourth time because we will repeat the lesson until we learn it.

Faith grows in this manner. Something comes that wrecks us. It could start as a lost friendship or job, moving to a new city, or the death of a pet or loved one, and we get the choice: to trust God in the situation. Will we have faith in his goodness through it all, even when the situation does not look so good?

Life is full of beautiful blessings and deep heartaches. You will continually experience both as you journey through life. The question is: the next time you experience heartache, will your faith in God's goodness and faithfulness grow stronger? He is faithful to help us through if we choose to turn to Him. "If we are faithless, he remains faithful—for he cannot deny himself" (2 Timothy 2:13, ESV)

People are wonderful, except when they are not quite so wonderful. A harsh comment, an unkind look, or the hundredth dreaded traffic jam, and suddenly we find it hard to love others. Love begins to feel like a burden. All of a sudden, love is something we must labor over until it happens in our heart.

Matthew 5:43-47 (ESV) reads, "You have heard that it was said, 'You shall love your neighbor and hate your enemy.' But I say to you, love your enemies and pray for those who persecute you, so that you may be sons of your Father who is in heaven. For he makes his sun rise on the evil and on the good, and sends rain on the just and on the unjust. For if you love those who love you, what reward do you have? Do not even the tax collectors do the same? And if you greet only your brothers, what more are you doing than others? Do not even the Gentiles do the same."

This scripture passage has brought me to my knees many times. The days I struggled to love those opposing me, God reminded me that when I show love, I am demonstrating his love. It is hard to love when you would rather not do so, which is why we must put effort behind love. We have to work at it, because loving others does not come naturally.

When we choose love in a situation in which another person expects us to react strongly, that person begins to wonder what is different about us. In those moments, we can respond with confidence that we are different because we love Jesus.

Lastly, let's look at the steadfastness of hope. "We have this hope as an anchor for the soul, firm and secure" (Hebrews 6:19, ESV). Crewmembers on a ship lower an anchor from a ship to keep it from drifting away from a desired location.

Anchors are strong and secure. They are made to not move in the heaviest storms. A good anchor connects the ship to the rocky sea floor instead of areas where sand covers the bottom. Like the ship's anchor, let us also anchor to Christ who is our rock, so that we may remain unwavering and steadfast in him.

"Everyone then who hears these words of mine and does them will be like a wise man who built his house on the rock. And the rain fell, and the floods came, and the winds blew and beat on that house, but it did not fall, because it had been founded on the rock. And everyone who hears these words of mine and does not do them will be like a foolish man who built his house on the sand. And the rain fell, and the floods came, and the winds blew and beat against that house, and it fell, and great was the fall of it" (Matthew 7:24–27 ESV).

Hope that is anchored in Christ will withstand any hardship. Storms will still form, but the Lord gives us safe passage through them, and he promises to walk with us in the midst of the storm.

The book of Titus began with Paul sharing why he was addressing Titus personally. "Paul, a servant of God and an apostle of Jesus Christ, for the sake of the faith of God's elect and their knowledge of the truth, which accords with godliness, in hope of eternal life, which God, who never lies, promised before the ages began and at the proper time manifested in his word through the preaching with which I have been entrusted by the command of God our Savior" (Titus 1:1–3, ESV).

Did you catch it? Paul told Titus to instruct God's people in knowledge of godly truth so that they might gain eternal life. Therein lies their hope—it is in eternal life. Since our hope lies in the "something better" God has promised, we have courage for today. We long to be with Jesus in Heaven where we will endure no more pain, no more suffering, and where many of our loved ones are. By putting our faith in Christ and living to please him, we know that one day we will arrive in Heaven.

We can find a third passage that refers to faith, hope, and love in 1 Thessalonians 5:8 (ESV), "But since we belong to the day, let us be sober, having put on the breastplate of faith and love, and for a helmet the hope of salvation."

Faith, hope and love are pieces of armor we use to protect ourselves, as we stand firm against the attacks of the enemy. The devil desires to keep us from the One who loves us most. We can take a stand against the evil one because, as Christians, we already have the victory.

I found the following passage in Ephesians, wrote it on a piece of paper, and taped it above my bed. Every morning, I read this and physically gird myself with the invisible armor found in Ephesians 6:10–18 (NIV), "Finally, be strong in the Lord and in his mighty power. Put on the full armor of God, so that you can take your stand against the devil's schemes. For our struggle is not against flesh and blood, but against the rulers, against the authorities, against the powers of this dark world and against the spiritual forces of evil in the heavenly realms. Therefore put on the full armor of God, so that when the day of evil comes, you may be able to stand your ground, and after you have done everything, to stand. Stand firm then, with the belt of truth buckled around your waist, with the breastplate of righteousness in place, and with your feet fitted with the readiness that comes from the gospel of peace. In addition to all this, take up the shield of faith, with which you can extinguish all the flaming arrows of the evil one. Take the helmet of salvation and the sword of the Spirit, which is the word of God. And pray in the Spirit on all occasions with all kinds of prayers and requests. With this in mind, be alert and always keep on praying for all the Lord's people."

Put on your armor so you can stand firm against the attacks of the evil one. Everywhere you walk today, bring his peace with you by the way you interact with others. Put your faith in God and his goodness, and the devil's threats will hold no ground.

By choosing salvation over death, you have already become God's precious child, and he is watching over you wherever you go. Use what God has given you in his word. Hebrews 4:12 (ESV) says, "For the word of God is living and active, sharper than any two-edged sword, piercing to the division of soul and of spirit, of joints and of marrow, and discerning the thoughts and intentions of the heart."

You have access to this! Memorizing scripture is the best way to have your sword, or the Word of God, readily available when you need it, although, any time spent in the Word helps us remember it, and God is so mighty that he can bring anything we have learned to the forefront of our memory when the situation arises.

Lastly, but equally as important: *pray!* Talk with God as you go to work, when you are putting your child down for his or her nap, and whenever you think of someone. God loves to commune with us, but he will not force us to talk with him. Communing with the Creator of the universe is a mere thought or spoken word away. How often we forget how close he really is.

Faith, hope, and love are virtues that always increase. There are not enough "good deeds to perform" that could reach the full capacity of the true, perfect love. Another way to say this is, sometimes people believe that good deeds will get them into Heaven instead of having a relationship with Jesus. Even if someone tried to do "good deeds" with the most genuine love for another, they would still fall short.

Love must first come from above and then fill us and heal us, and then we can pour out love freely. 1 John 4:19 (ESV) says, "We love because He first loved us." God's love is fulfilling.

When we are filled, we can pour out, but who can pour out of an empty tank? God gives us his love freely because we are his children, and so, as children, we are called to share his love as equally and as freely as he does. First John 3:1 (ESV) says, "See what kind of love the Father has given to us, that we should be called children of God; and so we are."

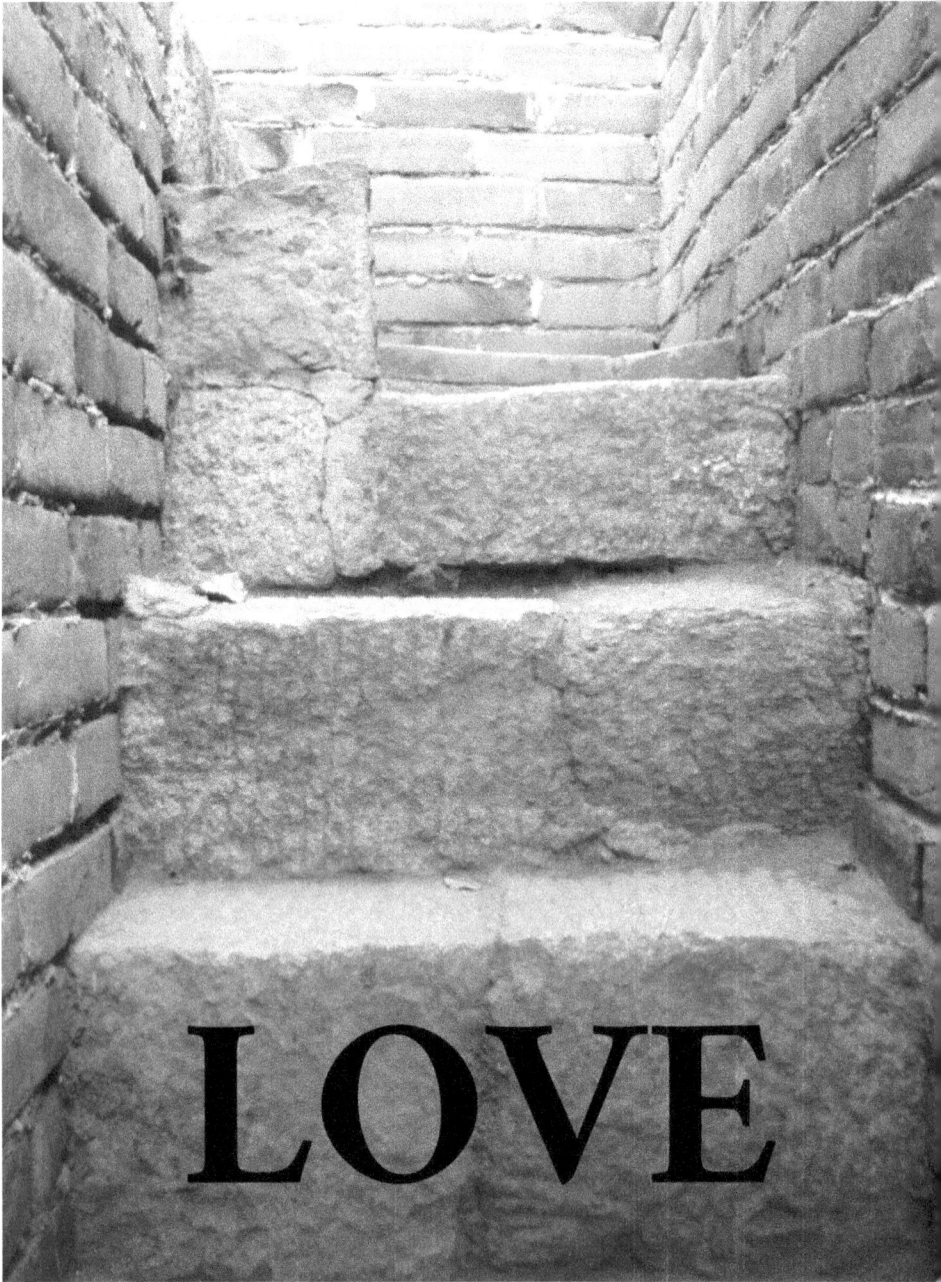

LOVE

CHAPTER 1

Love: Where We Start

Picture three stone blocks. One of them is massive, one is rough around the edges, and the last one shows cracks from being broken and pieced back together with mortar.

These three blocks come together to form the steps on my staircase; the journey of my Christian life. The massive block was the hardest one for me to step onto and is one I continue to work on daily. This large block on my staircase is love.

The rough stone represents the stair step that was the most painful for me to climb: hope. The smaller block, which is pieced back together, represents faith in my staircase.

Think about your staircase. Which step has been harder to climb atop? Which one was easier? Is there a chipped or mended one?

Sometimes the Lord will give us a word he wants to teach us about. Almost everywhere we look or everything we read seems to focus around the word or phrase God has put on our hearts.

One of the first words God taught me about was the word love. In fact, he is still teaching me. I have found we continue to grow in each of these three attributes—love, hope, and faith—during every day of our faith walk. We can always find more to learn about faith, hope, and love.

Each day we come into contact with other people, and we get to choose whether or not we will show them love. We make the choice to live each day for the Lord and walk in faith. We chose to have hope in God and his everlasting goodness because we know that on our own without that hope, we'd never have the courage to face tomorrow.

As I mentioned, the largest block in my staircase represents love. Perhaps this is the case for you too. I am continuing to grow in love. As long as we are with other people, we are learning more about love. Being around other believers helps us by having a supportive group to encourage us though the trails. Proverbs 27:17 (ESV) puts it this way, "Iron sharpens iron, and one man sharpens another."

Ever since the very beginning of time, humans were created to experience fellowship. God said in Genesis 2:18 (ESV), "It is not good that the man should be alone."

I tend to lean towards being introverted, and I crave a few minutes of unwinding from a busy day when I've spent time with others. I love being with others and spend most of my days with my community and the body of Christ. However, if I can spend a few minutes alone recharging my mental and emotional batteries, I am energized to go back out and spend more time with others again.

Whether or not we lean towards being introverted or extroverted, we are still called to fellowship with the body of believers. If you are like me and tend to be introverted, set a time to refresh and then set time to be around others too.

Each year I have a physical examination and then spend a few minutes going over my blood work results with health care professionals. They ask all the standard questions including, "How are you feeling?" or "How has your mood been?"

After the brunt of the COVID-19 pandemic, my health care professional mentioned that most of the people who worked from home felt a significant increase in depression and anxiety than those who did not.

People are social beings. We need to be with each other from time to time. Truthfully, in many professions people can work from home, which is better for themselves and their situations. If a person works from home, then he or she would be wise to also seek community and fellowship outside of the home.

We need balance between working for the Lord and spending time with him. Mary and Martha discovered this when they had a very important dinner guest, Jesus, himself! Their story is found in Luke 10: 38–42 (ESV). "Now as they went on their way, Jesus entered a village. And a woman named Martha welcomed him into her house. And she had a sister called Mary, who sat at the Lord's feet and listened to his teaching. But Martha was distracted with much serving. And she went up to him and said, 'Lord, do you not care that my sister has left me to serve alone? Tell her then to help me.' But the Lord answered her, 'Martha, Martha, you are anxious and troubled about many things, but one thing is necessary. Mary has chosen the good portion, which will not be taken away from her.'"

How can we love someone we do not know? Imagine this:

"Grandma is in town! Yes, Grandma Jenkins, and she's accepted the invitation to come to our home for thanksgiving this year! What an honor.

"Oh—she's coming in half an hour? We did not have time to cook a turkey this morning. Looks like ham it is! I hope she likes ham.

"What about the sweet potato casserole? It needs more marshmallows— everyone likes marshmallows.

"Millie, grab the sweeper! We haven't vacuumed yet! Millie, help me with these dishes, they won't clean themselves.

"She's here? Oh, so soon. Millie, get the door. I have too much to do. The pie isn't ready yet; stall her, Millie! I need help with these cups.

"Millie? Millie did you sweep the floor yet? Oh, Grandma Jenkins, thank you for coming! Sorry the house is a mess. Millie, aren't you going to come and help me? Grandma, tell her that I need some help. This dinner won't serve itself.

"What was that, Grandma? Millie chose the better portion? But I did all of this for you."

As Grandma Jenkins sat on the couch, she said, "But Sarah, you have ignored me the whole time I was here. I do not want your food or pristine service; I just want you. I want to spend time with you."

Grandma Jenkins in this story is like Jesus; he comes to spend time with you and would rather visit with you than experience a spotless kitchen.

What about you? Has your Bible become a rare artifact, collecting dust upon your shelf? What about your prayer life? Have you been spending time with God in prayer?

Having a relationship with Christ is ongoing. We do not just accept him into our lives and then ignore him once he's made himself at home. Similar to the story of Millie and Sarah above, we have invited a friend into our homes and then ignored him the entire time he is here.

If we have invited the Lord into our lives, the relationship does not end there. He wants to talk with us and hear from us and help us. Additionally, if we do not read the Bible or talk to him, then how will we know what he desires?

First and foremost, God loves us. 1 John 4:19 (ESV) says, "We love because he first loved us." God has loved us from the beginning. "For you formed my inward parts; you knitted me together in my mother's womb" (Psalm 139:13, ESV). He is our loving Creator, carefully piecing our likes, talents, interests, and personality all together into a beautiful person.

When I was in college, my anatomy and physiology professor taught us about the protein molecule Laminin. Laminin is made up of three molecules forming the shape of a cross. The Laminin molecule binds specific cells to membranes, and without it, our bodies would literally fall apart. Our Creator has literally knit our bodies together with the symbol of the cross. What a mighty God we serve!

God's love for us is greater than we can even imagine. The word love we use today has been watered down. We use the word love to describe our affection for a favorite dessert or even a preference for a specific sport.

In the original Greek translation of the Bible, four different words were used to differentiate the word love.

The first of these four words describing love is called *philos.* This is a friendship or a brotherly love for those you care about and the compassion you have towards your neighbor. I love my friends. We spend time hanging out and fellowshipping together. We often share meals together and encourage one another. Additionally, I've been fortunate to serve meals to those in need at a food pantry. I empathize with those who come seeking a meal, and we have some friendly conversation. I've met many amazing people in some hard situations and have been able to listen to their stories of hope and courage. I love them too.

Next, a husband and a wife share love for one another. They have fallen head over heels for each other and cannot wait to spend time together. Their passion grows deeper each day. They are falling in love more and more. This romantic love is the Greek word *eros.*

Additionally, every person on this earth has parents. From the moment parents first meet their child, they are typically filled with a great love. This love a parent has for their child continues until the child is older and grown. This is an affectionate love. This love is called *storge.*

Finally, the love God has for us is greater than all of these combined. God's unconditional love for us is called *agape.*

Let's look at God's *agape* love a little deeper. First Corinthians 13:4–8 (NIV) tells us what love looks like, "Love is patient, love is kind. It does not envy, it does not boast, it is not proud. It does not dishonor others, it is not self-seeking, it is not easily angered, and it keeps no record of wrongs. Love does not delight in evil but rejoices with the truth. It always protects, always trusts, always hopes, always perseveres. Love never fails." God loves us perfectly.

Humans were created with the capacity for love. We usually try to fill the empty places with *eros, philos,* or *storge* love, but nothing fills in the hole in our heart like *agape*. God loves us in our incompleteness, and he helps us in our situations when we repent, or ask for forgiveness of our sins, and call out to him. Psalm 23:5 (ESV) says, "you anoint my head with oil; my cup overflows."

Coffee drinkers know all too well how quickly the bottom of their cup appears after a short night. Seems like there is never enough coffee left in the cup. It quickly becomes time to fill the cup back up again and get recharged to head out for our workday. Our spiritual lives can reflect this need for a recharge or second cup as well.

Come with me to the coffee house of love. Jenny and Sally each hold a coffee cup for love to be poured inside by the Father. As they turn to the Lord, he fills their cups with love until the cup is full to the brim.

Jenny decides to leave the coffee house of love and go about her day. As she walks along, she sees another person coming along with a not-so-full cup, and then Jenny decides to share a little love gifted to her from the Father. Her love-level decreases a little, but nothing too concerning, and so she continues.

As Jenny gifts the godly love, which was first shared with her, to others the cup becomes less and less full. When she realizes she is now the one who is in need, she returns to the Lord to receive another abundant serving of love.

Now Sally also filled her cup in the coffee house of love, but she stayed in the corner, protecting her love. After Jenny returned for a refill, she saw Sally in the corner of the coffee house and went to talk with her friend. As they talked, she noticed Sally's love had soured since the love had sat in her cup for so long.

Jenny tried to add a little godly love to Sally's cup, but found Sally's cup was filled and unable to take in any more godly love. Then Sally left the coffee house of love to go about her day but found she couldn't pour from her cup. The liquid had soured and sat in molded clumps in the bottom of her cup. She turned over her cup and the once-godly love fell to the ground with a *plop!*

Sadly, Sally turned to Jenny for some Godly love refill, but as soon as the godly love touched the soured remains, the whole cup soured.

Jenny encouraged Sally to return with her to the Father at the coffee house of love to see what the Lord could do. Sally joined Jenny and they walked back together. Once inside, Sally explained that she had let her cup sour and she couldn't share from her cup anymore, then she and asked the Father if he could do anything for her cup of soured love.

Smiling, the Lord picked up her outstretched cup and cleaned it in the sink. When the soured stains were washed away, he poured a fresh batch of love into Sally's cup. She left the coffee house of love rejoicing and pouring out of her cup of godly love to anyone she met.

Jenny looked inside her coffee-stained cup and then looked to the Father, asking, "Is there any way I could get a fresh cleansing too?"

With a smile, the Father picked up her cup and cleaned it too. Then he filled the cup to overflowing, and Jenny raced outside to catch up with Sally.

Only one true love can fill our cups to overflowing, and this is the love of the Lord. Godly friendships are a blessing, and just like in this story of Sally and Jenny, godly friendships help us along the journey. However, no one can pour from an empty cup.

Our times of worship and talking with God and reading his word will refill our cups with godly love, and then we are ready to go out and share his love with others.

We face a danger if we withhold love from others. Withholding love will lead to a sour heart, which is hard to pour love out of. . Eventually, those around us will not be able to add love to our cups because we've allowed them to be full of sour bitterness instead. Thankfully, we serve a loving God who will forgive us when we repent of our sins, and he will refill our lives with his overflowing love once again. At that time, we will be able to willingly receive love again from those we love and who love us.

The following scripture strengthened the foundation of my faith when I was a child: "For God so loved the world, that he gave his only

Son, that whoever believes in him should not perish but have eternal life. For God did not send his Son into the world to condemn the world, but in order that the world might be saved through him. Whoever believes in him is not condemned, but whoever does not believe is condemned already, because he has not believed in the name of the only Son of God" (John 3:16–18, ESV).

As a child, I attended a private school where we were taught Christian and educational foundations. I was extremely shy and struggled with making friends. On my recesses, instead of playing with the other kids, I always found a quiet place and pulled out a small, bright orange, Gideon Bible, which contained the New Testament, Psalms, and Proverbs.

My favorite place to read was the front of this Bible where John 3:16 was printed in multiple languages. I was amazed at how many different languages I found. At a young age, I knew people all across the world were learning about God, just as I was doing.

John 3:16 and later verses 17–18, became my favorite passage of the Bible. For God so loved *me* that he gave his only Son, that if I believe in him I should not perish but have eternal life.

I carried this foundational scripture with me, even through the long days of a time when I ran away from God. *How could God love me?* I wondered during that time and in various times since then. Yet, he does. Just like he loves you, too.

After I rededicated my life to God, some of the things I learned about him are: he is majestic, omnipotent, omniscient, and omnipresent. Another way to say that is: God is great, all-powerful, all knowing, and everywhere present.

It is hard to hear these descriptions of God being everywhere present and all knowing and to know that within this large earth, he loves each of us uniquely. Our God is so vast that sometimes we find our minds cannot comprehend him, and this can feel overwhelming. Learning about the great, overwhelming love of God can be too much for our finite minds to understand. Whenever I try to comprehend his majesty, I am speechless because my earthly mind cannot comprehend the all-powerful, all knowing and everywhere present abilities of God. It is impossible to understand all of God's ways. Isaiah 55:9 (ESV) says, "For as the heavens are higher than the earth, so are my ways higher than your ways and my thoughts than your thoughts."

God has used several mentors who have spoken encouragement to me when I am astonished over God's immensity. One mentor has profoundly told me she thinks simply, "God loves me and that is all that matters. Whatever he says to do, I will do and I don't concern myself with the rest."

Another mentor shared with me what her mother used to tell her— she had a family member who was caught up on Bible trivia, but the person was not very kind. This woman knew whom so-and-so's fifth grandparent from the Bible was and was very well versed in biblical facts and knowledge. However, my friend's mother once said, "But what about the 'Beatitudes'? Are you living out those?" She was referring to Jesus' words in Matthew 5:2–12.

We can get caught up on knowing scriptural facts. But we have not truly learned scripture unless it becomes a reflection in our lives. God is the author of the Bible. He knows what the Bible says. He wants to know how much of it is found in you. He wants to know how much of it you are living out in your life.

The Bible refers to a holy reverential fear of the Lord. One of my favorite references to the fear of the Lord is found in Job 28:28 (ESV), "And he said to man, 'Behold, the fear of the Lord, that is wisdom, and to turn away from evil is understanding.'"

Another of my favorite references is in Proverbs 1:7 (ESV), "The fear of the Lord is the beginning of knowledge; fools despise wisdom and instruction."

These two scriptures help me understand the meaning behind the fear of the Lord better. The Lord is our Father, and as our Father, he disciplines and guides us.

When we were children, when our parents told us "no" to something, we might not have understood why they were telling us "no," but we learned to respect them and understand we could not do or have whatever we were asking for.

As we got older, we realized their answers tended to be for our best interest. Our parents taught us the stove was hot and we should not touch it and that we should look both ways before crossing the road, because they loved us and wanted to protect us. If we did not listen, we could get burned or killed.

If we respect and obey our earthly parents, how much more should we obey our heavenly Father? Hebrews 12:5–6 (ESV) explains this well, "And have you forgotten the exhortation that addresses you as sons? 'My son, do not regard lightly the discipline of the Lord, nor be weary when reproved by him. For the Lord disciplines the one he loves, and chastises every son whom he receives.'"

The Lord sees us as his sons and daughters. Some of us may not have had both parents growing up. Some may have not had fathers and mothers who were easy to love. When we choose to see God as our loving father, we experience the joy and love that comes from him. He fills those empty places and holds us when we cry out to him in our pain and sorrow. Once we are filled with the Father's love, we are able to turn and pour love into the hardest relationships.

If we struggle to show love to a parent, remember we have also messed up and need God's hand upon us to lead us. Once we go to the Lord and he strengthens us, we are able to love them with a pure heart.

Of all the Ten Commandments given to Moses, only one includes a promise. Exodus 20:12 (ESV) says, "Honor your father and your mother, that your days may be long in the land that the Lord your God is giving you."

Healthy, loving relationships between parents and children will look different from family to family. Talk with the Lord about how to best love your hardest-to-love family members. Sometimes he leads us to redemptive relationships, and sometimes we are led to healthy boundaries. Either way, God still says, "honor." Honor in the way you speak, the way you think, and the way you represent them to others. Each of us is to give an account of our actions one day, and we will be sharing about our own behavior and not that of others.

We have learned the Lord is our loving father, and he has our best interest at heart even when we cannot comprehend it. But, how do we learn to love him? Remember Job 28:28 (ESV)? "And he said to man, 'Behold, the fear of the Lord, that is wisdom, and to turn away from evil is understanding.'"

We find wisdom, knowledge, and the understanding of God and his ways through reading the Bible and praying. We cannot turn away from evil if we do not recognize what is sinful. We learn to love God by growing in wisdom. Another way to look at this is to see that we are learning to love God with our minds.

Mark 12:28-31 (ESV) "And one of the scribes came up and heard them disputing with one another, and seeing that he answered them well, asked him, 'Which commandment is the most important of all?' Jesus answered, 'The most important is, "Hear, O Israel: The Lord our God, the Lord is one. And you shall love the Lord your God with all your heart and with all your soul and with all your mind and with all your strength." The second is this: "You shall love your neighbor as yourself." There is no other commandment greater than these.'"

This scripture lists three ways we grow in loving God. The first we looked at was loving God with our minds.

The next way we are going to look at is how to grow in loving God with our hearts. To love God with our heart is to desire to pursue a relationship with him. We can often become caught up in religious practices and miss that the Lord desires a relationship with us instead. We can be caught up in religion over relationship in a few different ways.

We can get caught up in religious guidelines, which often are based on good intentions. For example, having candles, prayer shawls, and specific traditions in services can encourage the believer, but if the individual's heart is not in it for the Lord, all of these things can end up being ritualistic regulations. We must keep in check the intentions of our hearts. Religion focuses on the outside and the visible works we do, while pursuing a relationship with God is focused on the inside. God cares about the intentions of our heart.

Instead, we must pursue God-focused time in scripture, prayer and worship. These are fundamental for a believer because this is where we fellowship with God. "For he satisfies the longing soul, and the hungry soul he fills with good things" (Psalm 107:9, ESV).

Every time I go to the Lord when my soul is weary, he lifts me up and gives me strength. Sometimes I am unable to speak any words, and I just cry out to him. God hears my cry when I humble myself before him with a sincere heart. "Likewise the Spirit helps us in our weakness. For we do not know what to pray for as we ought, but the Spirit himself intercedes for us with groanings too deep for words" (Romans 8:26, ESV).

Friend, he also hears your cry when you earnestly seek him. The hardest days teach us to cling to our mighty God. Choose to go to him time and time again. Choose to actively seek the Lord and his will for your life. Choose a relationship with Christ.

Lastly, in order to grow in loving the Lord, we need to love the Lord with all of our soul. This means being completely devoted to God. Hebrews 4:12 (ESV) says, "For the word of God is living and active, sharper than any two-edged sword, piercing to the division of soul and of spirit, of joints and of marrow, and discerning the thoughts and intentions of the heart."

This verse shows the Holy Spirit who dwells in us is different than our soul. The Holy Spirit is God dwelling within us. He is our counselor and comforter.

Our soul is what makes us who we are individually. Our soul is made up of our talents, dreams, feelings, and personality. It is part of what makes us human, and because of this, we often have to remind our soul to keep in step with the Spirit. Paul referred to this inner struggle in Romans 7:15–20 (ESV), "For I do not understand my own actions. For I do not do what I want, but I do the very thing I hate. Now if I do what I do not want, I agree with the law, that it is good. So now it is no longer I who do it, but sin that dwells within me. For I know that nothing good dwells in me, that is, in my flesh. For I have the desire to do what is right, but not the ability to carry it out. For I do not do the good I want, but the evil I do not want is what I keep on doing. Now if I do what I do not want, it is no longer I who do it, but sin that dwells within me."

One of my favorite parts of this passage is in verse fifteen, where Paul said, "But I do the very thing I hate." The very thing Paul hated was sin. We should hate sin. The devil tries to dress up sin as pleasing to the eye. We can become tempted by our fleshly desires if we view sin as attractive.

As a believer in Christ, we are to put off our old self, as described in Ephesians 4:22–24 (ESV), "Put off your old self, which belongs to your former manner of life and is corrupt through deceitful desires, and to be renewed in the spirit of your minds, and to put on the new self, created after the likeness of God in true righteousness and holiness."

One way to avoid the temptations of the flesh is to downright hate them. Hate sin. Hate evil. Hate adultery. Hate stealing. Hate lying. Hate coveting. Hate the flesh temptations the devil throws at you personally.

Growing up, I was taught that hate was a strong word. In those childhood times, I used the word hate loosely and often used it to refer to dislikes I had. This included loved ones who did something I disliked.

So, I then tried getting around using the word by saying, "I strongly dislike." But truthfully, I did not strongly dislike my loved ones. I was just upset over what they did because it was different than what I thought was right.

We should not hate the person committing the sin. We can remind ourselves that we, too, have sinned and fallen short. The repentant thief still desires grace and love. Many times, the love shared from a caring friend helps lead someone to the feet of Jesus.

Once the devil knows something bothers us, he will try to tempt us with any chance he gets. Because we know the Lord and have the Holy Spirit as our guide, we can find the way out of temptation safely. First Corinthians 10:13 (ESV) says, "God is faithful, and he will not let you be tempted beyond your ability, but with the temptation he will also provide the way of escape, that you may be able to endure it."

The Lord is not the source of our temptations, the devil is. We build perseverance when we make the right choice time and time again, and we become stronger to turn away from temptations coming our way. This happens over time, and we are continually growing in choosing the right choices for the rest of our lives.

Review Questions:

- What do your blocks of faith, hope, and love look life? Is one rougher with chips? Cracked? A huge stone? What do your building blocks look like?
- Has your Bible become a rare artifact collecting dust on your shelf? What about your prayer life?

Scripture memory verse:

1 Corinthians 13:4–8 (NIV)

"Love is patient, love is kind. It does not envy, it does not boast, it is not proud. It does not dishonor others, it is not self-seeking, it is not easily angered, and it keeps no record of wrongs. Love does not delight in evil but rejoices with the truth. It always protects, always trusts, always hopes, always perseveres. Love never fails."

Challenge:

You have been given a cup full of love from the Father; find someone you can share his love with this week.

CHAPTER 2

Love: As We Grow

Many years ago, I worked at a large retail store. I enjoyed the work, but I struggled with showing love to the customers. Few were satisfied, and the fitting rooms were always atrocious. Most of my day was dedicated to working at the register or in the fitting room, and I learned a few things about people during that time. First, you must check the fitting room after every person. Sometimes, people brought everything out, yet other times the clothes were left in a wadded-up heap.

Truly, it does not matter how a person leaves their fitting room—although I felt like a mom or a servant while picking up after other people. However, if I had not felt this way, I would not have been able to accept the wonderful scripture I clung to during this time. Psalm 84:10 (ESV) says, "For a day in your courts is better than a thousand elsewhere. I would rather be a doorkeeper in the house of my God than dwell in the tents of wickedness."

One day! Just a single day in the presence of God is so vastly better than a thousand days anywhere else! I would rather be a servant watching the door than to be living in wickedness apart from God's presence.

I would repeat this scripture as I walked to each room, knowing that even if I felt like a servant, I was already a servant of the Lord. I could do my best in any job as long as he was walking with me.

Second, I learned many people love money. They really do. Paul was correct when he shared in 1 Timothy 6:10 (ESV), "For the love of money is a root of all kinds of evils. It is through this craving that some have wandered away from the faith and pierced themselves with many pangs."

It was difficult when a coupon expired, and I needed to relay that information to the customer. We should remember our actions when we talk with one another. Our words should be kind, even when things are not going as we think they should. We should be conscious on saving money, but we should refrain from loving money. Both Luke 16:13 (ESV) and Matthew 6:24 (ESV) share, "No servant can serve two masters, for either he will hate the one and love the other, or he will be devoted to the one and despise the other. You cannot serve God and money."

One of my friends was in a difficult place of wanting to help everyone and feeling overwhelmed by this burden. Another friend of mine told him we should help the people God brings before us, such as the family who lives down the street and cannot afford Christmas gifts this year. The man you pass on the side of the road who is holding a cardboard sign. The missionaries at your church who are about to go off on a mission trip.

God places people before us, and then he is the one who speaks to our heart on whether or not we are to give. We cannot help everyone, and sometimes we are actually the ones who need help.

I have been in hard times where I dug my pocket change out to put one more gallon of gas in my car so I could make it to the next paycheck. Several times I have received the blessing of a friend who bought my meal for me. I have also had the opportunity to do so for others.

The first time someone outside of my family bought a meal for me, I broke down in tears. I had enough money for the meal, but it was an extra expense I had not budgeted for. I tried to refuse, and they told me, "Don't deny us a blessing."

This changed my life. There is joy in giving (2 Corinthians 9). When we give, we not only pass on a blessing, but we also receive one as well.

You see, we are to bear each other's burdens, but we are also told to be wise with money as the "Parable of the Talents" found in Matthew 25:14–30 (ESV) shows us:

For it will be like a man going on a journey, who called his servants and entrusted to them his property. To one he gave five talents, to another two, to another one, to each according to his ability. Then he went away. He who had received the five talents went at once and traded with them, and he made five talents more. So also he who had the two talents made two talents more. But he who had received the one talent went and dug in the ground and hid his master's money. Now after a long time the master of those servants came and settled accounts with them. And he who had received the five talents came forward, bringing five talents more, saying, "Master, you delivered to me five talents; here, I have made five talents more." His master said to him, "Well done, good and faithful servant. You have been faithful over a little; I will set you over much. Enter into the joy of your master." And he also who had the two talents came forward, saying, "Master, you delivered to me two talents; here, I have made two talents more." His master said to him, "Well done, good and faithful servant. You have been faithful over a little; I will set you over much. Enter into the joy of your master."

He also who had received the one talent came forward, saying, "Master, I knew you to be a hard man, reaping where you did not sow, and gathering where you scattered no seed, so I was afraid, and I went and hid your talent in the ground. Here, you have what is yours." But his master answered him, "You wicked and slothful servant! You knew that I reap where I have not sown and gather where I scattered no seed? Then you ought to have invested my money with the bankers, and at my coming I should have received what was my own with interest. So take the talent

from him and give it to him who has the ten talents. For to everyone who has will more be given, and he will have an abundance.
But from the one who has not, even what he has will be taken
away. And cast the worthless servant into the outer darkness. In
that place there will be weeping and gnashing of teeth."

How are you using your talents? In addition to times of financial
blessing, you have also been given talents of spiritual gifts from God.
Romans 12:4–8 (ESV) tells us, "For as in one body we have many members, and the members do not all have the same function, so we, though
many, are one body in Christ, and individually members one of another. Having gifts that differ according to the grace given to us, let us
use them: if prophecy, in proportion to our faith; if service, in our serving; the one who teaches, in his teaching; the one who exhorts, in his
exhortation; the one who contributes, in generosity; the one who leads,
with zeal; the one who does acts of mercy, with cheerfulness."

Love others with the gifts God has given you. You may feel the urge
to help homeless people or nursing homes or children or someone who
is close to you. Maybe you are a wonderful baker or your carpentry skills
are always spot on. God blesses the talents you use for him, because he is
the one who gave them to you in the first place. God sees, and he placed
the longing in your heart to help others.

Since I was a child, one of my deepest longings was to visit China.
One day my dream became my reality. I experienced an amazing opportunity to go on a mission trip to China. I was nervous since I had neither
flown nor left the country. One night, I was up late talking with God
about whether or not I should go. I was listening to music and the song
"Do Something" by Matthew West played. The song talks of the trouble
in the world. There are poor people and children exploited and it can be
easy to turn to God to ask him what he is doing about it. Then God says,
I did do something; I made you. I made you to go and help them. I made
you to shine the light of Jesus in their life. You feel this burden for these

people, so will you answer the call to go and help them? God made you and me and gave us this desire to help them. This song asks, will you go and help them?[iii]

While listening to this song, I received my confirmation from the Lord to go on the mission trip. It was the greatest adventure of my life. I had been called to go, and God opened the door. This came about through a conversation with someone I barely knew. I was telling her that I'd wanted to see China since I was a young girl. The woman heard my heart-cry and invited me to go with her church.

On our trip, I learned that they had led mission trips to China for almost thirty years. I got to witness firsthand her love for the people around the world and see their dedication to share Jesus with people all around the world. God sure knows how to put the right people in your life at the right time. This sweet friend showed me how to love others by how she genuinely loved the Lord and wanted to share this love with everyone she met even unto the ends of the earth. Maybe your calling is not overseas, just maybe it is next door, where you can have the same impact in your neighborhood as missionaries overseas. You can share the gospel with your neighbor, like the missionaries are sharing with their neighbors in other countries. Wherever God calls you, He will equip you, and then He will grow you through it.

Romans 12:9–21 (ESV) shows us the signs of the true Christian:

> Let love be genuine. Abhor what is evil; hold fast to what is good. Love one another with brotherly affection. Outdo one another in showing honor. Do not be slothful in zeal, be fervent in spirit, serve the Lord. Rejoice in hope, be patient in tribulation, be constant in prayer. Contribute to the needs of the saints and seek to show hospitality. Bless those who persecute you; bless and do not curse them. Rejoice with those who rejoice, weep with those who weep. Live in harmony with one another. Do not be haughty, but associate with the lowly. Never be wise in your own sight.

Repay no one evil for evil, but give thought to do what is honorable in the sight of all. If possible, so far as it depends on you, live peaceably with all. Beloved, never avenge yourselves, but leave it to the wrath of God, for it is written, "Vengeance is mine, I will repay, says the Lord." To the contrary, "if your enemy is hungry, feed him; if he is thirsty, give him something to drink; for by so doing you will heap burning coals on his head." Do not be overcome by evil, but overcome evil with good.

Learning about love is the mere starting place. Every day, love has the opportunity to grow, if we tend to it. We can display the marks of a true Christian and still be growing in them. Many of us may hold jobs and lifestyles that are not exactly what we dreamed of when we were younger. My friend, God is in those too.

My retail job was not my dream job, and some days I struggled to love my customers. However, this was the very tool God used to teach me about love. Some days I would be so angry looking at the endless piles of clothes needing put away that I would think, *But I hate them. How can I love them? How can I love someone I really don't want to love?* And God had a verse for those thoughts.

First John 2:9–11 (ESV) says, "Whoever says he is in the light and hates his brother is still in darkness. Whoever loves his brother abides in the light, and in him there is no cause for stumbling. But whoever hates his brother is in the darkness and walks in the darkness, and does not know where he is going, because the darkness has blinded his eyes."

If you choose hate over love, you are just the same as if you had never accepted Christ at all. I want to clarify this: *If you choose to hate your brother or sister, you are no better off than if you had never accepted Christ in the first place.*

Can you imagine?

I had accepted Jesus in my life and turned my life over to him. But, choosing not to love the people he placed before me was like saying I did not even love Jesus at all. I was heartbroken and told the Lord I did love him.

Every time I told him I loved him, he reminded me of my customers. These were the people in my sphere of influence. I had the ability to show the life-changing love of God to them. God revealed to me that I could not show the life-changing love of God until I was first filled with it myself.

Spending time in prayer and the Word is pivotal. Imagine with me that you have a best friend whom you love dearly. Nevertheless, when that person comes over to visit, you choose to ignore him or her. That person sits on your couch eagerly waiting to speak to you. After all, you invited him or her over so you could spend the day together.

Now, picture Jesus there. You invited him into your life, but you cannot remember the last time you talked with him. You placed your scripture reading on the back burner. I understand. It is so hard to juggle life.

One ball representing family, another work, and yet another your personal life, and there is still another to pick up. What are your priorities?

When we put God as first, everything else will always fall into place. If we claim to love God more than anything and as our top priority, then our actions should prove it.

Love seemed impossible for me to grasp. I honestly had no idea where to start in showing love to others; all I knew was that God was telling me to love them. You see, once God calls you to something, he beings to teach you about it. Often, the way we learn to love best is by applying scripture in experiences.

The Lord gave me this scripture in 2 Peter 1:5–10 (NASB), "Now for this very reason also, applying all diligence, in your faith supply moral excellence, and in your moral excellence, knowledge; and in your knowledge, self-control, and in your self-control, perseverance, and in your perseverance, godliness; and in your godliness, brotherly kindness, and in your brotherly kindness, love. For if these qualities are yours and are increasing, they render you neither useless nor unfruitful in the true knowledge of our Lord Jesus Christ. For he who lacks these qualities is blind or short-sighted, having forgotten his purification from his former sins. Therefore, brethren, be all the more diligent to make certain about His calling and choosing you; for as long as you practice these things, you will never stumble"

Start the journey now with putting your faith in Jesus Christ, but then watch as your faith grows into love. No matter when you start, keep going! Choose to grow into the deep depths of God's love.

I started at the bottom: *Okay Lord, I have faith, now I will choose to do good and think good thoughts like Philippians 4:8 (ESV) references.* "Finally, brothers, whatever is true, whatever is honorable, whatever is just, whatever is pure, whatever is lovely, whatever is commendable, if there is any excellence, if there is anything worthy of praise, think about these things."

This ties into the next step: knowledge. Memorize scripture. Scripture is the best defense against the enemy, and he will try to discourage and tempt us to try to defeat us. The times we are weakest, he tries to belittle us. Fight back as Jesus did with his knowledge of scripture (Matthew 4:1–11).

There is a difference between using scripture because the verse sounds right and using scripture to equip and encourage ourselves. The Holy Spirit reveals the scriptures to us as we read. Let us start our time in the Word with an open heart and a simple prayer: "Lord, open my eyes to what you are revealing to me in your Word."

By learning the scriptures and pursuing moral excellence, or goodness as some translations use, we learn self-control. Self-control is the ability to walk away from temptation. The next time we face temptation, we can remember we have the "the sword of the Spirit, which is the word of God" (Ephesians 6:17, ESV) to fight back with.

Each time we choose to fight against temptation, the next time becomes easier as we develop self-control. Now, a desire builds in our hearts to persevere. We are now determined to walk with God and know he will not let us down because we have tested his words for ourselves and persevered through the trials and know he never failed us.

The next step was the hardest for me because I struggled to see myself as having godliness or holiness. God is holy; this was easy to see. But me? I struggled to see how I could have any holiness. I still fell down and faltered. I am not perfect. It took a different perspective to grasp godliness. First Corinthians 6:19-20 (ESV) reads, "Or do you not know that your body is a temple of the Holy Spirit within you, whom you have from God? You are not your own, for you were bought with a price. So glorify God in your body."

God's presence in us, through the Holy Spirit, is the source of godliness. We cannot claim it ourselves, for we can do nothing "good enough" to become godly. A believer's time in the Word is revealed in the godliness stage. We are imperfect people loved by a perfect God who knows we are not perfect. This is why he gave us Jesus to come and save the world.

However, Paul warned in Romans 6:1–4 (ESV) of believers continuing to sin because God's grace provides a safety net. "What shall we say then? Are we to continue in sin that grace may abound? By no means! How can we who died to sin still live in it? Do you not know that all of us who have been baptized into Christ Jesus were baptized into his death? We were buried therefore with him by baptism into death in order that, just as Christ was raised from the dead by the glory of the Father we too might walk in newness of life."

Because we accepted Jesus in our hearts, the Lord gives us the Holy Spirit as our guide. As a result, the Holy Spirit's presence in our hearts, thoughts, and actions reveals his godliness within us.

The next step to love is brotherly kindness. By having godly responses and genuinely caring for our neighbors, we become kind to one another. This is simple, but can be made complicated. Look for ways to reach out to other people. Do you know of anyone in need? Does your neighbor need his grass mowed? Is your church sharing food with the community? Do you have knitting skills you can use to create stockings for the children's Christmas play? Maybe you have different talents or abilities? You can invite other people over for a meal and a Bible Study. Invite someone over who needs a listening ear instead of an advice-filled conversation. And if you don't have the physical abilities for these outreaches, you can always, always pray. In fact, praying is one of the greatest acts of love you can do for someone else.

So, if these are all demonstrations of loving others, why are these listed with brotherly kindness instead of under love? Have you ever helped someone because you knew it was the right thing to do, but your heart wasn't quite in it? You were being kind to them, but love is with the heart, not just the actions. Love is your heart and actions coming together as you care for others. People can tell the difference between love in action and kindness in action. Love goes beyond a kind action because the receiver feels it.

By all means, continue in kindness, for this leads to your heart to follow. Finally, we radiate God's love. We have learned to listen for the Holy Spirit's nudging. We have become diligent to look for others who need help and reach out as best as we can to help them.

God blesses us when we love others. He says, "Give, and it will be given to you. Good measure, pressed down, shaken together, running over, will be put into your lap. For with the measure you use it will be measured back to you" (Luke 6:38, ESV). My beloved friend, you cannot out give God.

A Christian is revealed in how they choose to respond differently than most people, often times, causing them to stand out. "You are the light of the world. A city set on a hill cannot be hidden. Nor do people light a lamp and put it under a basket, but on a stand, and it gives light to all in the house. In the same way, let your light shine before others, so that they may see your good works and give glory to your Father who is in heaven" (Matthew 5:14–16, ESV).

Again, faith, hope, and love are always increasing in a believer's life. When we meet new people or difficult situations come up, we can remember 2 Peter 1:5–10 and follow the steps to get back to genuinely loving people again.

There is no limit to how much God can pour out his love over us, so we have no limit on how much we can also love others. Fill your cup with personal time spent loving God, and you will never run dry.

No longer will you be desperate for others to fill you with love, because God fills you to overflowing. When you are filled with love, you can love others appropriately, without seeking anything from them in return. We have the same mission Paul gives to Timothy in 1 Timothy 1:5 (ESV), "The aim of our charge is love that issues from a pure heart and a good conscience and a sincere faith."

Jesus says in John 15:12–13 (ESV), "This is my commandment, that you love one another as I have loved you. Greater love has no one than this, that someone lay down his life for his friends."

Jesus proved his love for us by dying on the cross to give us eternal life. After I decided to go on a mission trip to China, I met some missionaries. I began eagerly telling them about my upcoming adventure. I shared about how I had always dreamed to see China, and I was going to fly on an airplane and leave the country for the first time in my life.

Unfazed by my excitement, a middle-aged man from the group looked me straight in the eye and asked, "Are you willing to die for Jesus?"

I was taken aback because no one had ever asked me this question. I thought deeply about his question and responded with a truth-filled, "Yes."

Finally, he smiled and said, "Then that is all that matters."

That was all that mattered? Yes, really. It does not matter how many mission trips you have taken to other countries. It does not matter how many people were in your church service last week. It does not matter if you minister to the same group of people under the same roof each day. None of those factors makes you more equipped than others.

It does not even matter how many people you have influenced for Jesus, if you did not reach out to them out of pure intentions. What matters is your heart, and if you are reaching out to others out of love for Jesus. If you are willing to say, "Yes Lord, wherever you send me I will go because it means I am going with you. No matter the cost I choose you because I love you too."

This does not mean you are constantly entering life-threatening situations. This means today, in the here and now, you will choose his plan and follow his leading.

If you do not love the Lord and are trying to do good deeds to fill your soul up instead of their coming from fellowshipping with him, this is like taking a stock pot and filling it with water and then either green beans, corn-on-the-cob or chicken. Once the water boils off, you are left with the good stuff.

When trials come into your life—and my friend, they surely will—all the water boils off due to the intensity of the heat. Did you put enough good stuff in there? Will you have much chicken left in the bottom to feed your family? How much Christ-likeness is left in the bottom of your stockpot? Have you been communing and fellowshipping with God? Because when it boils down to it, we want Jesus to be what is left in the bottom of our stockpot after all of the water has boiled off.

Only God knows when the time has come for us to go home, and he will prepare us. Even though we commit to being prepared to die for Christ, if it becomes called for, God alone knows the exact time for us to come home. Our responsibility is to be prepared, so we will make it bravely to the end of our lives, clinging to the Lord.

Peter thought he was ready, but Jesus knew he was not prepared yet. John 13:36–38 (ESV) reads, "Simon Peter said to him, 'Lord, where are you going?' Jesus answered him, 'Where I am going you cannot follow me now, but you will follow afterward.' Peter said to him, 'Lord, why can I not follow you now? I will lay down my life for you.' Jesus answered, 'Will you lay down your life for me? Truly, truly, I say to you, the rooster will not crow till you have denied me three times."

Luke 22:31-34 (ESV) also shares this same encounter, "'Simon, Simon, behold, Satan demanded to have you, that he might sift you like wheat, but I have prayed for you that your faith may not fail. And when you have turned again, strengthen your brothers.' Peter said to him, 'Lord I am ready to go with you both to prison and to death.' Jesus said, 'I tell you, Peter, the rooster will not crow this day, until you deny three times that you know me.'"

In his heart, Peter was ready. He was certainly passionate about Jesus and believed he would choose to die for him. When the time came to test Peter's words, something faltered. Perhaps in his mind, he was afraid and saw death was imminent. Or perhaps his heart weakened, and he chose to save his life, as many people would when they face death. Whatever the reason, Jesus knew Peter was not ready yet.

But the amazing part comes next when Jesus encouraged Peter so he would be ready someday. Notice what Jesus said, he "prayed for you that your faith may not fail. And when you have turned again, strengthen your brothers" (v. 32).

Jesus already knew Peter would deny him, and he knew Peter would turn back again. Jesus prayed for Peter to not turn his back entirely on believing in Jesus as the Son of God. Peter had been the first disciple to admit Jesus was the Son of God in Matthew 16:16–18 (ESV), "Simon Peter replied, 'You are the Christ, the Son of the living God.' And Jesus answered him, 'Blessed are you, Simon Bar-Jonah! For flesh and blood has not revealed this to you, but my Father who is in heaven. And I tell you, you are Peter, and on this rock I will build my church, and the gates of hell shall not prevail against it.'"

After Jesus rose from the dead, he spoke with Peter in John 21:15–19 (ESV), and Jesus tested Peter three times to see if he genuinely loved Him. Peter confessed to loving Jesus, and Jesus gave him the mission to tend to the flock Jesus had gathered.

Peter was eventually crucified for following Jesus, as foretold in verses 18–19, "'Truly, truly, I say to you, when you were young, you used to dress yourself and walk wherever you wanted, but when you are old, you will stretch out your hands, and another will dress you and carry you where you do not want to go.' (This he said to show by what kind of death he was to glorify God.) And after saying this he said to him, 'Follow me.'"

Peter laid down his life for his friend both figuratively and literally, and in doing so, he proved his love and commitment for Jesus.

If you haven't already, now is a great time to search your heart with the Lord (Psalm 139:1–3, ESV). Will you choose to give each day over to God? Be on the lookout, for he is calling you to love the people in your circle of influence. You get to choose who you will serve, just as Joshua purposed to the Israelites, "And if it is evil in your eyes to serve the Lord, choose this day whom you will serve, whether the gods your fathers served in the region beyond the River, or the gods of the Amorites in whose land you dwell. But as for me and my house, we will serve the Lord" (Joshua 24:15, ESV).

Review Questions:

- In what ways are you using or planning to use the talents and Spiritual gifts God has given you?
- What are your priorities? Who is at the top of your list? Is the Lord asking you to change any of your priorities?

Scripture memory verse:

2 Peter 1:5–7 (NASB)

"Now for this very reason also, applying all diligence, in your faith supply moral excellence, and in your moral excellence, knowledge, and in your knowledge, self-control, and in your self-control, perseverance, and in your perseverance, godliness, and in your godliness, brotherly kindness, and in your brotherly kindness, love."

Challenge:

Find someone you can bless this week; whether financially, with a card or homemade gift, help with a project, or in another creative way.

CHAPTER 3

Love: Where We Are Heading

The love of God is greater far
Than tongue or pen can ever tell;
It goes beyond the highest star,
And reaches to the lowest hell;
The guilty pair, bowed down with care,
God gave His Son to win;
His erring child He reconciled,
And pardoned from his sin.
O love of God, how rich and pure!
How measureless and strong!
It shall forevermore endure
The saints' and angels' song.
Could we with ink the ocean fill,
And were the skies of parchment made,
Were every stalk on earth a quill,
And every man a scribe by trade,
To write the love of God above,
Would drain the ocean dry.
Nor could the scroll contain the whole,
Though stretched from sky to sky.

The Love of God was written by Frederick M. Lehman in 1917. When he reached the third verse, he struggled to come up with words. "At length, he thought of some lines he had recently heard in a sermon:

Could we with ink the ocean fill and were the skies of parchment made,

Were every stalk on earth a quill, and every man a scribe by trade,

To write the love of God above would drain the ocean dry,

Nor could the scroll contain the whole though stretched from sky to sky.

"That verse perfectly formed the third stanza, but who had written it? As Frederick heard the story, it was composed on the wall of an insane asylum by an unknown inmate."[iv]

There is no greater example of love than the Lord himself. His love for us is immeasurable. By Jesus's death our sins were buried, and by his resurrection, we rise to new life in him. We cannot comprehend this. How could or how would, a perfect, sinless, holy, all-powerful God, humble himself to become a man? For him to live a perfect life, by fulfilling the law and taking our sin unto himself, then choosing to die to set us free from sin and be resurrected so we could have eternal life and live with him forever, it begs us to ask the age-old question, "Why?" The answer? "Love."

As the song says, to be able to write the love of God would drain the ocean dry. We cannot understand it, but we can accept his love for us and love him in return.

The Bible is packed full of stories of people whom God loved and of those who loved him. God loves his people. He always has. He has given them second and third and fourth and even hundredth chances. The Lord is a God of mercy, grace, and forgiveness. In the Old Testament, His people were the Israelites. In the New Testament, his people were those who believed in his Son, Jesus Christ.

First of all, Jesus is the ultimate example of loving the Father. Jesus is God's Son sent to earth to redeem us from our sins and give us eternal life. "And when Jesus was baptized, immediately he went up from the water, and behold, the heavens were opened to him, and he saw the

Spirit of God descending like a dove and coming to rest on him; and behold, a voice from heaven said, 'This is my beloved Son, with whom I am well pleased'" (Matthew 3:16–18, ESV).

Throughout the New Testament, Jesus led by showing people how to love the Father and each other. Jesus always had time for others, and he also sought out alone time with his Father, even if it meant getting up well before dawn as described in Mark 1:35 (ESV), "And rising very early in the morning, while it was still dark, he departed and went out to a desolate place, and there he prayed."

Jesus continually put the Father's will and desires above his own. And he prioritized spending time with his heavenly Father. Prayer is an act of love. It is an ongoing conversation with God. Jesus gave us an example on what prayer looks like in Matthew 6:9–13 (NASB). "Pray, then, in this way: 'Our Father, who is in heaven, hallowed be Your name. Your kingdom come. Your will be done, on earth as it is in heaven. Give us this day our daily bread. And forgive us our debts, as we also have forgiven our debtors. And do not lead us into temptation, but deliver us from evil.'"

Jesus teaches us how to pray in this passage using key points.

Jesus starts with giving God the glory and asking the Father to do his will on earth just like he does in heaven. Then, he taught his listeners to pray for daily needs: food, water, shelter, all of the things we need daily to survive. By using the word daily, Jesus demonstrated that we would continue to pray for these needs each day. Instead of praying for riches, we are to pray for him to meet our needs.

Additionally, our great God knows what we need, and he cares for us and the things we want. I am thankful he has also answered many of my "wants" prayers. Coming to God daily in prayer is relying on and trusting him with all of our "needs," whether or not he fulfills our "wants."

We are also to ask for forgiveness for our sins and are reminded to forgive others who have sinned against us. Jesus elaborates on this further in Matthew 6:14–15 (NASB) "For if you forgive other people for their offenses, your heavenly Father will also forgive you. But if you do not forgive other people, then your Father will not forgive your offenses."

If we want to be forgiven, we also need to have a heart of forgiveness towards others.

Lastly, we ask the Lord to keep us from temptation and deliver us from evil. The devil hates God. He will do anything to disrupt God's plans and will, but he is powerless against God.

As humans, God gave us the freedom of choice. If we were without this freedom, then God would be a powerful dictator, forcing us to do whatever he wanted. But our loving God gave us this ability, and he gave us the option to choose him for ourselves, because he loves us. God will not force us to choose him; instead he lovingly offers all we could ever want and more.

The devil will try to keep as many people away from God as he can. He is the evil one. The devil is also the tempter. Matthew 4:1 (ESV) reveals this to us, "Then Jesus was led up by the Spirit into the wilderness to be tempted by the devil."

In the rest of this passage, we see Jesus was tempted three times by the devil. Once about food because Jesus had been fasting and was hungry. Another time, Jesus was tempted about displaying his power so all the people would immediately believe in him by seeing his great signs and wonders. And lastly, Jesus was tempted by the devil saying he would give the whole world to Jesus if Jesus bowed down to him. All three times, Jesus successfully fought against the devil with scripture.

Jesus may have been tempted by the devil, who was trying to influence his desires, but Jesus won the victory.

We too are tempted by the devil. We sin when we act upon the temptation, not when we face a temptation. Pray to God when tempted, for prayer is the pathway to escape the temptation. "No temptation has overtaken you that is not common to man. God is faithful, and he will not let you be tempted beyond your ability, but with the temptation he will also provide the way of escape, that you may be able to endure it" (1 Corinthians 10:13, ESV).

Prayer is conversing, like we talk with a friend. Sometimes it looks like the Lord's Prayer, at other times it is a quick, "Help me, Jesus" prayer.

Either way, the more you pray and talk with God, the easier prayer becomes. Jesus is recorded to have prayed for several hours in the Garden of Gethsemane on the night before his arrest, which later led to his crucifixion. He also invited his disciples to pray with him. Jesus knew the disciples would have their faith tested the next day and was trying to lead them to be prepared.

In Mark 14:37–38 (ESV), Jesus asked his disciples why they could not stay awake for an hour to pray. "And he came and found them sleeping, and he said to Peter, 'Simon, are you asleep? Could you not watch one hour? Watch and pray that you may not enter into temptation. The spirit indeed is willing, but the flesh is weak.'"

We are to have a prayerful mind throughout the day and keep our thoughts pointing to the Lord. Sometimes we are tired, like Peter was. At other times, we are distracted. The Holy Spirit helps us with this, and he gently guides our minds back when we drift away as we reach out to him. As believers, we are like the disciples in the garden. We are near the Lord, but we will falter when our faith is tested if we do not reach out to him and prepare ourselves by keeping watch with a prayerful mind. Could we, too, keep watch in prayer for an hour?

Later, in John 17, Jesus prayed for all of his disciples both present with him and the future ones who will come to know the Lord. "I am not asking on behalf of these alone, but also for those who believe in me through their word, that they may all be one; just as you, Father, are in me and I in you, that they also may be in us, so that the world may believe that you sent me. The glory which you have given me I also have given to them, so that they may be one, just as we are one; I in them and you in me, that they may be perfected in unity, so that the world may know that you sent me, and you loved them, just as you loved me" (John 17:20–23, NASB).

Jesus prayed for future generations. He prayed for you and for me.

I have been blessed by grandparents who prayed with us often when my siblings and I were growing up. We prayed on our way to school. We prayed at night before bed. We prayed at church. We prayed before meals. But the most special prayers were the ones I heard them say at night after they left our bedrooms and went to pray in their room.

I could hear them pray for my siblings and me by name, and they prayed for our future. When I was in my teens and became distant from God, I still knew deep down in my heart that my grandparents were praying for me.

Prayer is an act of love. Prayer cannot be curtailed. The devil cannot stop prayer. The only way he can touch prayer is if he can convince you not to pray.

Take Jesus' example and pray for the next generation. Prayers do not die when we do. Deuteronomy 7:9 (ESV) says, "Know therefore that the Lord your God is God, the faithful God who keeps covenant and steadfast love with those who love him and keep his commandments, to a thousand generations."

Have you ever thought of your prayers reaching to a thousand generations to come? Pray for your grandparents, your great-grandparents, your parents, your aunts and uncles, your cousins, your siblings, your nieces and nephews, your kids, your grandkids, your great-grandkids, and your future descendants who will come from them. Pray for them all and trust them in God's mighty hands. Bring those you love in prayer before the One who loves them the most.

But, do not stop there. Pray for someone's salvation. Pray for the ambulance with its lights on that just passed by you on the highway. Pray for wisdom and discernment for doctors. Ask God to do a mighty work in someone's life. Pray for your friends. Pray for the stranger you just met. Pray for an unbeliever to come to know Christ.

Pray for the kids of an unbeliever. And after you've prayed for them, choose to pray with them. There is only one way to find out if they would pray with you; ask. Ask, "Can I pray for you?" And then pray aloud with them what is on your heart.

As 1 Thessalonians 5:17 (ESV) says, "Pray without ceasing." Be ready to pick up a conversation with the Lord at any point throughout the day. Prayer is conversing with God.

I did not begin praying aloud until a few years after I rededicated my life to God. Praying out loud was overwhelming at first, but the Lord guided me through. Often, I pray silently before I pray aloud, asking the Lord to guide my words and give me the words to say.

Whether we pray aloud or quietly, we should talk to God as a friend. We pray with reverence and respect for him, as we would respect our parents. As we grow in this, the Holy Spirit will help us and teach us what to say, but we must be committed to continue in prayer. If we stop communing with God, we stop growing in our relationship with him.

Something that has been helpful to me is to start praying to the Lord silently, then when I am called upon to pray aloud, I am prepared and already in the conversation.

Where do we pray? We can pray anywhere! However, prayer should never be a show. "But when you pray, go into your room and shut the door and pray to your Father who is in secret. And your Father who sees in secret will reward you. And when you pray, do not heap up empty phrases as the Gentiles do, for they think that they will be heard for their many words. Do not be like them, for your Father knows what you need before you ask him" (Matthew 6:6–8, ESV).

Many years ago, I set aside a place in my closet to pray. This is where I spend most of my longer, consecutive prayer times. Often, I will also pray silently at work. At other times, I will pray aloud with people in public places. Wherever we pray, it is a conversation between God and us. As the previous scripture warns, our focus should be entirely on God and not on impressing those around us.

Jesus not only loved the Father, but he also loved those around him. First John 4:8 (ESV) says, "Anyone who does not love does not know God, because God is love."

Jesus is the Son of God, and he is part of the trinity of the Father, Son, and Holy Spirit. Jesus performed countless signs and miracles during his time on earth, and all of them were performed out of love for the receiver.

Jesus came to earth for us. God sent his Son for us, because he loves us. First John 4:10–12 (ESV) shows us this, "In this is love, not that we have loved God but that he loved us and sent his Son to be the propitiation for our sins. Beloved, if God so loved us, we also ought to love one another. No one has ever seen God; if we love one another, God abides in us and his love is perfected in us." God is love and he desires to teach us to love.

Luke 6:27–38 (ESV) shows us further what love looks like,

But I say to you who hear, Love your enemies, do good to those who hate you, bless those who curse you, pray for those who abuse you. To one who strikes you on the cheek, offer the other also, and from one who takes away your cloak do not withhold your tunic either. Give to everyone who begs from you, and from one who takes away your goods do not demand them back. And as you wish that others would do to you, do so to them. If you love those who love you, what benefit is that to you? For even sinners love those who love them. And if you do good to those who do good to you, what benefit is that to you? For even sinners do the same. And if you lend to those from whom you expect to receive, what credit is that to you? Even sinners lend to sinners, to get back the same amount. But love your enemies, and do good, and lend, expecting nothing in return, and your reward will be great, and you will be sons of the Most High, for he is kind to the ungrateful and the evil. Be merciful, even as your Father is merciful. Judge not, and you will not be judged; condemn not, and you will not be condemned; forgive, and you will be forgiven; give, and it will be given to you. Good measure, pressed down, shaken together, running over, will be put into your lap. For with the measure you use it will be measured back to you.

Jesus used a story we call the Parable of the Good Samaritan to explain loving our neighbor. This passage is found in Luke 10:25–37 (ESV):

And behold, a lawyer stood up to put him to the test, saying, "Teacher, what shall I do to inherit eternal life?" He said to him, "What is written in the Law? How do you read it?" And he answered, "You shall love the Lord your God with all your heart and with all your soul and with all your strength and with all your mind, and your neighbor as yourself." And he said to him, "You have answered correctly; do this, and you will live." But he, desiring to justify himself, said to Jesus, "And who is my neighbor?"

Jesus replied, "A man was going down from Jerusalem to Jericho, and he fell among robbers, who stripped him and beat him and departed, leaving him half dead. Now by chance a priest was going down that road, and when he saw him he passed by on the other side. So likewise a Levite, when he came to the place and saw him, passed by on the other side. But a Samaritan, as he journeyed, came to where he was, and when he saw him, he had compassion. He went to him and bound up his wounds, pouring on oil and wine. Then he set him on his own animal and brought him to an inn and took care of him. And the next day he took out two denarii and gave them to the innkeeper, saying, 'Take care of him, and whatever more you spend, I will repay you when I come back.' Which of these three, do you think, proved to be a neighbor to the man who fell among the robbers?" He said, "The one who showed him mercy." And Jesus said to him, "You go, and do likewise."

Mercy, grace, forgiveness are all acts of love. These are all qualities we learn firsthand from our loving God.

Believers are not to pick favorites to show love towards and therefore shun others, as we find in James 2:1–13 (ESV):

My brothers, show no partiality as you hold the faith in our Lord Jesus Christ, the Lord of glory. For if a man wearing a gold ring and fine clothing comes into your assembly, and a poor man in shabby clothing also comes in, and if you pay attention to the one who wears the fine clothing and say, "You sit here in a good place," while you say to the poor man, "You stand over there," or, "Sit down at my feet," have you not then made distinctions among yourselves and become judges with evil thoughts? Listen, my beloved brothers, has not God chosen those who are poor in the world to be rich in faith and heirs of the kingdom, which he has promised to those who love him? But you have dishonored the poor man. Are not the rich the ones who oppress you, and the ones who drag you into court? Are they not the ones who blaspheme the honorable name by which you were called?

If you really fulfill the royal law according to the Scripture, "You shall love your neighbor as yourself," you are doing well. But if you show partiality, you are committing sin and are convicted by the law as transgressors. For whoever keeps the whole law but fails in one point has become guilty of all of it. For he who said, "Do not commit adultery," also said, "Do not murder." If you do not commit adultery but do murder, you have become a transgressor of the law. So speak and so act as those who are to be judged under the law of liberty. For judgment is without mercy to one who has shown no mercy. Mercy triumphs over judgment.

One day, judgment is coming for the good and sinful acts we have done. Since mercy triumphs over judgment, our sins are forgiven when we ask for forgiveness from the Lord with a repentant heart. On judgment day, we want to be counted with the sheep and not the goats of the world.

The Sheep and the Goats

When the Son of Man comes in his glory, and all the angels with him, then he will sit on his glorious throne. Before him will be gathered all the nations, and he will separate people one from another as a shepherd separates the sheep from the goats. And he will place the sheep on his right, but the goats on the left. Then the King will say to those on his right, "Come, you who are blessed by my Father, inherit the kingdom prepared for you from the foundation of the world. For I was hungry and you gave me food, I was thirsty and you gave me drink, I was a stranger and you welcomed me, I was naked and you clothed me, I was sick and you visited me, I was in prison and you came to me." Then the righteous will answer him, saying, "Lord, when did we see you hungry and feed you, or thirsty and give you drink? And when did we see you a stranger and welcome you, or naked and clothe you? And when did we see you sick or in prison and visit you?" And the King will answer them, "Truly, I say to you, as you did it to one of the least of these my brothers, you did it to me."

Then he will say to those on his left, "Depart from me, you cursed, into the eternal fire prepared for the devil and his angels. For I was hungry and you gave me no food, I was thirsty and you gave me no drink, I was a stranger and you did not welcome

me, naked and you did not clothe me, sick and in prison and
you did not visit me." Then they also will answer, saying, "Lord,
when did we see you hungry or thirsty or a stranger or naked
or sick or in prison, and did not minister to you?" Then he will
answer them, saying, "Truly, I say to you, as you did not do it to
one of the least of these, you did not do it to me.' And these will
go away into eternal punishment, but the righteous into eternal
life" (Matthew 25:31–46. ESV).

One of my favorite ways to enter into the presence of the Lord is
through song. As Psalm 100:4 (ESV) says, "Enter his gates with thanksgiving, and his courts with praise! Give thanks to him; bless his name!"

We have a lot to be thankful for and David is a great example of
thanking God in song. Second Samuel 22:1–4 (ESV) provides a great
example of this, "And David spoke to the Lord the words of this song on
the day when the Lord delivered him from the hand of all his enemies,
and from the hand of Saul. He said, 'The Lord is my rock and my fortress and my deliverer, my God, my rock, in whom I take refuge, my
shield, and the horn of my salvation, my stronghold and my refuge, my
savior; you save me from violence. I call upon the Lord, who is worthy
to be praised, and I am saved from my enemies.'"

David's rock and foundation was the Lord. We find that David wrote
many of the psalms, as he continually sang about the Lord. The Lord
loved David, and David loved the Lord with all his heart. Psalm 18:2
(ESV) talks of David loving God, "The Lord is my rock and my fortress

"To the choirmaster. A Psalm of David, the servant of the Lord, who
addressed the words of this song to the Lord on the day when the Lord
delivered him from the hand of all his enemies, and from the hand of
Saul. He said: I love you, O Lord, my strength."

In Acts 13:22, the scripture tells us that God referred David as a man
after his own heart, "And when he had removed him, he raised up David

to be their king, of whom he testified and said, 'I have found in David the son of Jesse a man after my heart who will do all my will.'"

What would God say of us? Does he hear from us in conversation? Are we willing to follow his will no matter what? Would he call us his friends? Are we praising him with a thankful heart? Would we, too, be referred to as a people after his own heart?

Another person in the Bible God specifically talks of loving is none other than David's son, Solomon. Second Samuel 12:24-25 (ESV), "Then David comforted his wife, Bathsheba, and went in to her and lay with her, and she bore a son, and he called his name Solomon. And the Lord loved him and sent a message by Nathan the prophet. So he called his name Jedidiah, [Jedidiah means beloved of the Lord] because of the Lord."

As Solomon aged, he too loved the Lord as found referenced in 1 Kings 3:3 (ESV)," Solomon loved the Lord, walking in the statutes of David his father, only he sacrificed and made offerings at the high places."

Solomon had a special encounter with God where the Lord gave him the opportunity to ask for anything he wanted. If the Lord came before us today saying he would give us something, what would we ask him for?

Solomon made an excellent choice and asked God to give him wisdom to correctly govern the Lord's people; the Israelites.

And the king went to Gibeon to sacrifice there, for that was the great high place. Solomon used to offer a thousand burnt offerings on that altar. At Gibeon the Lord appeared to Solomon in a dream by night, and God said, "Ask what I shall give you." And Solomon said, "You have shown great and steadfast love to your servant David my father, because he walked before you in faithfulness, in righteousness, and in uprightness of heart toward you. And you have kept for him this great and steadfast love and have given him a son to sit on his throne this day. And now, O Lord my God, you have made your servant king in place of David my father, although I am but a little child. I do not know how to go out or come in. And your servant is in the midst of your people whom you have chosen, a great people, too many to be numbered or counted for multitude. Give your servant therefore an understanding mind to govern your people, that I may discern between good and evil, for who is able to govern this your great people?"

It pleased the Lord that Solomon had asked this. And God said to him, "Because you have asked this, and have not asked for yourself long life or riches or the life of your enemies, but have asked for yourself understanding to discern what is right, behold, I now do according to your word. Behold, I give you a wise and discerning mind, so that none like you has been before you and none like you shall arise after you. I give you also what you have not asked, both riches and honor, so that no other king shall compare with you, all your days. And if you will walk in my ways, keeping my statutes and my commandments, as your father David walked, then I will lengthen your days" (1 Kings 3:4–14, ESV).

Solomon's downfall was mentioned in I Kings 3:3. Even though Solomon had wisdom, he chose to leave up the altars that people used to worship other gods because he had married women who worshipped those gods. This caused a divide for him and the Lord's people, and they turned away from God years later by worshipping the idols instead of the living God.

Thankfully, Solomon returned to God towards the end of his life, and he is believed to have written much of both Proverbs and Ecclesiastes, which are often referred to as the books of wisdom in the Bible.

May we, too, ask the Lord to give us wisdom to help us walk godly lives and not turn away from him to sin.

One of the most interesting recordings in the Bible of a person specifically called loved by God is the disciple John. Throughout John's gospel account, he repeatedly refers to himself as "the one whom Jesus loved."

One day my sister and I were talking about the Lord, and she asked me, "Why is John the one who Jesus loved? Doesn't he love everyone?" At the time, I did not know how to answer her, so I sought to discover why this was written in the Bible. I knew God "so loved the world" as found in John 3:16. I knew Jesus died to take away the sins of the world and give all of us a chance at new life. So, what did this passage mean for you and me?

John is thought of as one of Jesus' closest friends. He, along with Peter and James, went to places with Jesus where most of the other disciples did not go. All three of them were in the Garden of Gethsemane on the night Jesus was arrested. However, the book of John is the only place John is referred to as *the one whom Jesus loves.* In Mark 3:17 (ESV), Jesus calls John and his brother James something else entirely, "James the son of Zebedee and John the brother of James (to whom he gave the name Boanerges, that is, Sons of Thunder)."

"Sons of thunder" has a very different ring to it than "the one whom Jesus loved." *The NIV Zondervan Study Bible* says, "May indicate their propensity to react harshly to perceived opposition."[v]

This is another way to say they tended to have a temper. I believe John, himself, would have known this and recognized his ongoing struggle with his flesh, yet he chose not to focus on it. Instead, he focused on God loving him.

The study Bible also expands on who was "the disciple whom Jesus loved" by saying it was "probably John, the author of this Gospel. The expression does not mean that Jesus did not love the others; it may be the author's way to avoid giving even the impression of sharing a platform with Jesus. It also testifies to one disciple's profound sense of being loved by Jesus, even as it reminds readers that the author is an eyewitness of the events he recounts."[vi]

John saw firsthand many wonders and signs of God's glory. He could have bragged about it. He could have said, "I, John saw this or that because

I was a part of Jesus' squad." Instead, he chose to view himself just like everyone else: another person whom Jesus loved.

We are all loved by Christ, but do we take John's example and choose to see ourselves in this way? Instead of the "great one," the "broken one," the "passionate one," "the heartbroken one," the "strong one," "the one with a temper," the "intelligent one," or the "determined one" to instead be the "one whom Jesus loved, even through our imperfections."

Hope Bolinger shared this same thought in her article "Why is John the 'Disciple Whom Jesus loved'?"

"But John appears to draw the spotlight away from himself in the narrative by removing his name and putting in a nickname instead, a trait: someone loved by Jesus. Here he highlights the transformative power Jesus had over his life. Through God's love he finds truth, his identity, and his purpose. He reminds readers and himself that all disciples of Jesus are loved, truly, wholly, and unconditionally."

She also states, "Preacher Charles Spurgeon explained that Jesus clearly loved all of his disciples. After all, on the night in which He was betrayed, He washed all of their feet. Yes, even Judas Iscariot's."

We should all follow John's example and see ourselves as the ones Jesus loves. Hope adds a great point in her article, "We don't know the real meaning behind the name because John provides no explanation of it. But perhaps John uses this name as a reminder to himself and others of Jesus' loving ministry here on earth and the disciples' call to spread the message of that love to every nation."[vii]

The book of Daniel is one of my favorite passages in the Bible. He was a man who was faithful and dedicated to the Lord. In Daniel 10:19 (ESV), an angel called him "greatly loved."

Why was he greatly loved? Daniel repeatedly went before the Lord and sought God's heart, desires, and will, even in the face of death. "When Daniel knew that the document had been signed, he went to his house where he had windows in his upper chamber open toward Jerusalem.

He got down on his knees three times a day and prayed and gave thanks before his God, as he had done previously" (Daniel 6:10. ESV).

Daniel was not ashamed to be associated with God. He was not afraid to be called God's friend and follower, even if it would cost him his life. And so, God was not ashamed to acknowledge Daniel. Jesus said in Matthew 10:32–33 (ESV), "So everyone who acknowledges me before men, I also will acknowledge before my Father who is in heaven, but whoever denies me before men, I also will deny before my Father who is in heaven."

Just like Daniel, we should be faithful to follow God wholeheartedly. When we choose to follow Christ, it was not meant to be a light decision to take back whenever we wanted. "Whoever does not bear his own cross and come after me cannot be my disciple. For which of you, desiring to build a tower, does not first sit down and count the cost, whether he has enough to complete it? Otherwise, when he has laid a foundation and is not able to finish, all who see it begin to mock him, saying, 'This man began to build and was not able to finish.' So therefore, any one of you who does not renounce all that he has cannot be my disciple" (Luke 14:27-30, 33, ESV).

We may never experience a life-or-death situation like Daniel did. We may reach an old age before we die, but the question remains: Did we live for Christ? And even though one day we die physically, as believers, we have the gift of eternal life.

We are not on this journey alone. Jesus talked about the Holy Spirit in John 14:15–27 (ESV):

"If you love me, you will keep my commandments. And I will ask the Father, and he will give you another Helper, to be with you forever, even the Spirit of truth, whom the world cannot receive, because it neither sees him nor knows him. You know him, for he dwells with you and will be in you. I will not leave you as orphans; I will come to you. Yet a little while and the world will see me no more, but you will see me. Because I live, you also will live. In that day you will know that I am in my Father, and you in me, and I in you. Whoever has my commandments and keeps them, he it is who loves me. And he who loves me will be loved by my Father, and I will love him and manifest myself to him." Judas (not Iscariot) said to him, "Lord, how is it that you will manifest yourself to us, and not to the world?"

Jesus answered him, "If anyone loves me, he will keep my word, and my Father will love him, and we will come to him and make our home with him. Whoever does not love me does not keep my words. And the word that you hear is not mine but the Father's who sent me. These things I have spoken to you while I am still with you. But the Helper, the Holy Spirit, whom the Father will send in my name, he will teach you all things and bring to your remembrance all that I have said to you. Peace I leave with you; my peace I give to you. Not as the world gives do I give to you. Let not your hearts be troubled, neither let them be afraid."

The Holy Spirit is our comforter, friend, and guide. He also convicts us when we sin and reminds us to turn back to God. When we grow in our relationship with the Lord, we get to know the Holy Spirit's voice. The more we are in the Word and prayer, the better we become at discerning his voice.

Ask God for clarity in hearing the Holy Spirit's whisper. When we hear the Holy Spirit and choose our own evil desires over what he teaches, we quench his Spirit in us. The more we say "no" to God, the less we will hear him speak to us.

If we turn away, our hearts will harden. We will eventually have a "heart of stone" instead of a fleshly heart sensing the moving of the Holy Spirit. Allow your heart to be softened by the Lord by continually seeking him and his voice.

At the end of the day, we must choose: Are we going to accept the Lord's love and choose to love him in return, or will we turn away from him and choose to live with a hardened heart?

Review Questions:

- What does loving your neighbor look like?
- What does loving God look like?

Scripture memory verse:

Luke 10:27 (ESV)

"And he answered, 'You shall love the Lord your God with all your heart and with all your soul and with all your strength and with all your mind, and your neighbor as yourself.'"

Challenge:

Who can you pray for? Who should you add to your prayer list?

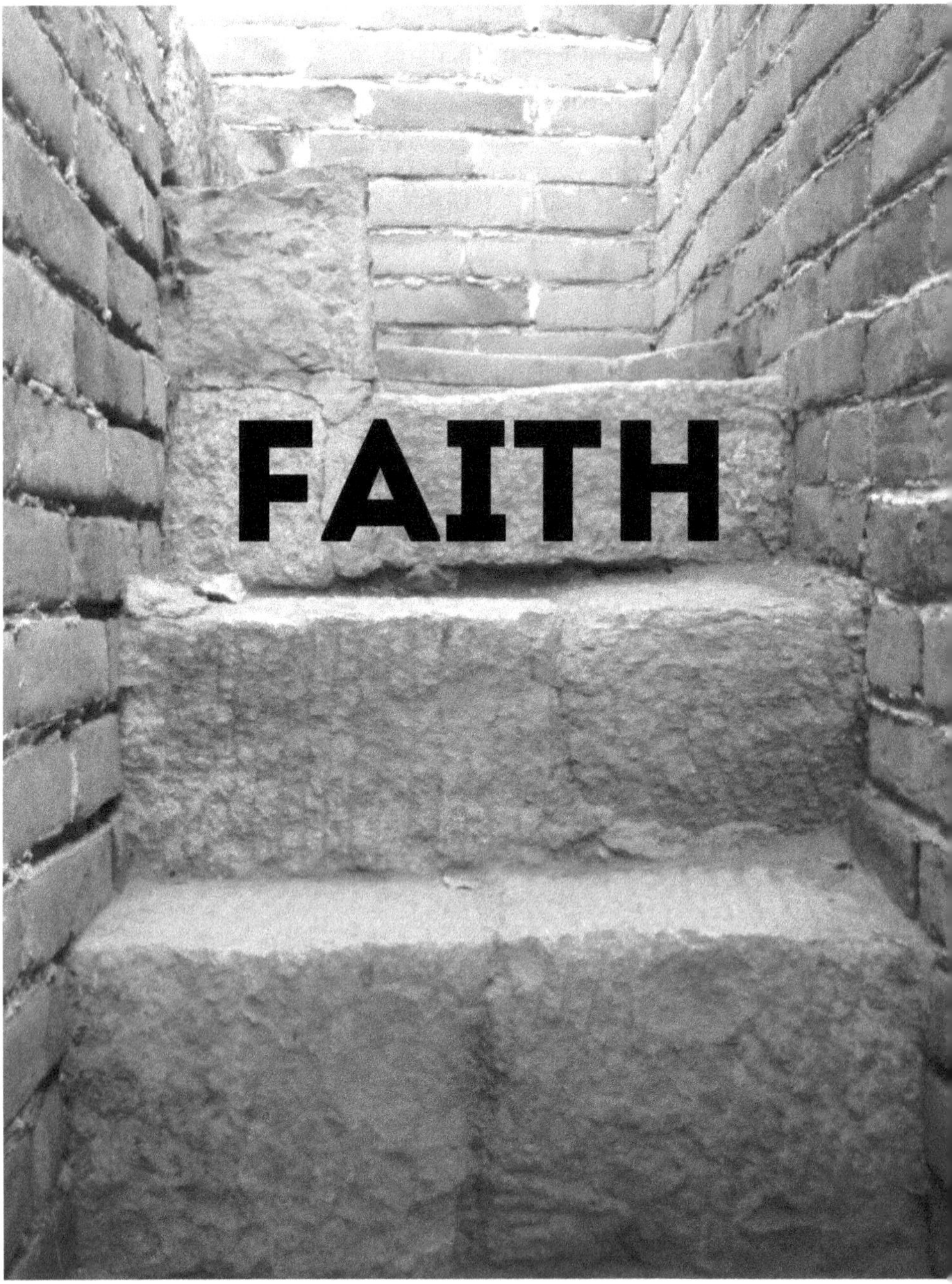
FAITH

CHAPTER 4

Faith: Where We Start

A young child lay in her "big girl bed" as her mom knelt beside her and prayed with her, as they tended to do each night. However, this time would be different. The mom asked the little girl if she wanted to accept Jesus into her life. The little girl agreed and the mom patiently led her daughter in prayer.

Step by step, through repentance, verbally professing Jesus is Lord, and believing within the heart, this became the night of my salvation.

Although this was my first step in my relationship with Jesus, so much more would come later. My childhood was spent attending church and learning about the Lord. When I reached junior high, my family and I moved to another state. The next eight years of my life were filled with worldly influences, sporadic church visits due to difficulty finding a home church, and ultimately a spiraling away from the Lord. By the time I reached college age, I was focused on doing things my way and had plastered a false smile over the growing depression deep in my heart.

The day before my nineteenth birthday, I went home from college for the weekend to celebrate with my family. I was dealing with losing a close friendship, several crucial and sinful choices, and feeling completely alone with no one to turn to.

How could I turn to the Lord when I had broken his heart and sinned against him? I had broken the promise I made as a young child. I was done. Done with life. Done with friends. Done with family.

After being awake for over thirty-six hours, I laid down in a bathtub with my face partially submerged under water and prepared to fall asleep. By the grace of God, my Memaw repeatedly knocked on the door and asked questions that required me to respond. Each time, I raised my head out of the water to answer her. After almost an hour of this, I gave up. We celebrated my birthday the next day, and life appeared to be repeating the same emptiness.

I returned to school, and that Monday night, I was listening to Christian music and reading my Bible. Suddenly, I felt the urge to walk to the prayer chapel on the Christian campus. At first I repeatedly dismissed the thought, but I finally gave in and walked to the chapel. Once inside, I sat on an empty pew and poured out my heart to God. That night I decided to rededicate my life to the Lord.

Each person needs to decide for himself or herself to commit to following Christ. Our parent's faith will not get us into heaven. We must choose on our own to not only accept the Lord into our lives, but to also commit to living daily for him. Ephesians 4:22–24 (ESV) puts it this way, "Put off your old self, which belongs to your former manner of life and is corrupt through deceitful desires, and to be renewed in the spirit of your minds, and to put on the new self, created after the likeness of God in true righteousness and holiness."

Choosing to accept Jesus in our hearts means deciding to put behind a life of sin and strive to walk in righteousness and the will of God.

Salvation is the starting place of faith. If you have never accepted Jesus into your life, and you are reading this book without that foundation, I want to encourage you to accept him. It is the most life-changing decision I ever made, and I can guarantee it will change your life, too.

God calls us and stirs our hearts towards him. "Then he told them many things in parables, saying: 'A farmer went out to sow his seed. As he was scattering the seed, some fell along the path, and the birds came and ate it up. Some fell on rocky places, where it did not have much soil. It sprang up quickly, because the soil was shallow. But when the sun came up, the plants were scorched, and they withered because they had no root. Other seed fell among thorns, which grew up and choked the plants. Still other seed fell on good soil, where it produced a crop—a hundred, sixty or thirty times what was sown. Whoever has ears, let them hear'" (1 Corinthians 13:3–9, NIV).

The Lord plants seeds of the gospel for us to discover as we journey the path of life. Sometimes he uses tools like scripture on a canvas picture you saw in passing at the mall. He can catch your eye with a book. Or maybe a friend spoke to you and demonstrated the love of God. Or maybe he used your parents.

As believers who have accepted Christ, we are helping scatter the seeds of the gospel as 1 Corinthians 3:6–7 (ESV) tells us, "I planted, Apollos watered, but God gave the growth. So neither he who plants nor he who waters is anything, but only God who gives the growth."

We can scatter seeds of the gospel, but we cannot make someone accept the Word. We can only offer it as the solution they are seeking.

As the Parable of the Sower explained, sometimes the trials of life will quickly take away the seeds. At other times, a person may not let seeds take deep root in their hearts, and when the trials come, the person will wither under the pressure. In other instances, the pleasures of this world will choke out the seed of the gospel. Lastly, sometimes the gospel will fall on awaiting ears that will cling to God no matter what comes.

When the storms of life come, will the seed be washed away, eaten by birds, choked by thorns, or lost its footing in deceptively shallow sand? Or will our soul be nurturing so that the seed could grow and thrive?

When the scattered seeds of the gospel come into our lives, we want it to take root. We want to grow bountifully in the Lord and that starts with our salvation. Sometimes we hear bits and pieces of the gospel before we accept the Lord. We might have heard that Jesus died on the cross for our sins but maybe we had not heard that Jesus died for the sin of the whole world. Let's look at salvation together.

In the book of Romans, we find a powerful way to explain salvation in five verses that form what is referred to as the Romans Road. "What is the Romans Road to salvation? The Romans Road to salvation is a way of explaining the good news of salvation using verses from the Book of Romans. It is a simple yet powerful method of explaining why we need salvation, how God provided salvation, how we can receive salvation, and what are the results of salvation." The Romans Road is comprised of Romans 3:23, Romans 6:23, Romans 5:8, Romans 10:9–10 and Romans 5:1.[viii]

Step one of the Romans Road is found in Romans 3:23 (ESV), "For all have sinned and fall short of the glory of God." Each person has sinned. Every single person. Doing "good" things does not make someone a "good" person. Those positive deeds cannot purify the heart. If we become tempted to compare ourselves to another who appears to have himself or herself together, we need to remember this verse. Not one person is without sin except Jesus. When we realize this, we can move on to the next step.

Romans 6:23 (NIV) tells us, "For the wages of sin is death, but the gift of God is eternal life in Christ Jesus our Lord."

Now that we understand that everyone has sinned, we see that sin leads to death. Sinning earns death. When God created Adam and Eve, they would have never experienced death until sin entered the world through their choices (See Genesis 3). Before we blame Adam and Eve for all of the sin in the world, we need to remember that we are just as guilty of sin as Adam and Eve. We have also chosen to sin.

The human race would have been hopeless, except God had a plan. Someone needed to die for our sins because sin separates us from a holy God and brings death. So the Father sent his only Son to die for our sins in our place. As believers, even though our bodies will die on this earth, our spirit will not die. Through Jesus, we have received the gift of God, the promised eternal life.

This leads us to Romans 5:8, (ESV), "But God shows his love for us in that while we were still sinners, Christ died for us."

I love this verse. *While we were sinners*, Christ died for us. He did not die for the cleaned-up version that came afterwards. He died for the unkind, hateful, rude, selfish, sinful person we are without him. John 15:3 (ESV) puts it this way, "Greater love has no one than this, that someone lay down his life for his friends."

He calls us his friends when we do not deserve it. God loves us so much that he did all of this for me and for you. He would have done it all just for you to bring you home. "What do you think? If a man has a hundred sheep, and one of them has gone astray, does he not leave the ninety-nine on the mountains and go in search of the one that went astray? And if he finds it, truly, I say to you, he rejoices over it more than over the ninety-nine that never went astray" (Matthew 18:12–13, ESV).

From cover to cover of the Bible, we see God picking the down and out, the least of these, the smallest lineage of their family, the youngest in the line-up. All of these were ones that no one else would have picked. They all had humble and lowly beginnings, much like Jesus' own entrance into the world.

Jesus came as a baby to a small lineage, to a generational line of the ones-chosen-last, to be born in a stable and laid in a manger, also referred to as a feeding trough. (Luke 2). This was supposed to be a great king. The Jews anticipated the Lord's mighty one that was going to change the world. What they received instead was a seemingly helpless baby.

However, that "helpless baby" did change the world. Jesus had small beginnings just like us. He chooses the weak and the humble. They are the ones who say, "Lord, I cannot do this on my own. I need you." They are the ones that recognize it is not by their might but by the Lord's.

"Here I am! I stand at the door and knock. If anyone hears my voice and opens the door, I will come in and eat with that person, and they with me" (Revelation 3:20, NIV) He is here! The Lord stands at the door of our hearts and knocks.

Many churches have displayed an old picture of Jesus knocking at a door. On the famous painting, you can see that the doorknob is not on the outside where Jesus stands. This is to symbolize that the Lord never forces open the door, but he patiently waits for us to open it. While this scene has been depicted in different ways by different artists, in some depictions, weeds grow high around Jesus' feet. This shows that he has been out there knocking for a long time. Is he still standing outside the door of your heart too? Or, have you opened the door to him and welcomed him in?

How do we welcome Jesus in and become saved? Romans 10:9–10 delves into this, "If you confess with your mouth that Jesus is Lord and believe in your heart that God raised him from the dead, you will be saved. For with the heart one believes and is justified, and with the mouth one confesses and is saved."

Confess Jesus is Lord and believe in your heart, and you will be saved. My friend, there is a great rejoicing over every sinner that comes homes.

"Now the tax collectors and sinners were all drawing near to hear him. And the Pharisees and the scribes grumbled, saying, 'This man receives sinners and eats with them.' So he told them this parable: 'What man of you, having a hundred sheep, if he has lost one of them, does not leave the ninety-nine in the open country, and go after the one that is lost, until he finds it? And when he has found it, he lays it on his shoulders, rejoicing. And when he comes home, he calls together his friends and his neighbors, saying to them, "Rejoice with me, for I have found my sheep that was lost." Just so, I tell you, there will be more joy in heaven over one sinner who repents than over ninety-nine righteous persons who need no repentance'" (Luke 15:1–7, ESV)

Jesus took on the sin of the world and left it at the cross. When Jesus rose from the grave, the sin was not on him anymore. John 19:30 (ESV) says, "When Jesus had received the sour wine, he said, 'It is finished,' and he bowed his head and gave up his spirit."

The work he came to do was finished. Through his death and resurrection from the dead three days later, Jesus paved a way for us to have forgiveness and a way to restore our broken relationship with our Father in Heaven. All we have to do is believe in Jesus and that he died and rose again to save us from our sins.

The last leg of the Romans Road is Romans 5:1 (ESV), "Therefore, since we have been justified by faith, we have peace with God through our Lord Jesus Christ."

Now, we have peace with the Lord. The sin, which was a barrier to our having a direct relationship with God, has been removed.

Peace is a powerful gift that the Father grants to us. Peace comes from having faith in God and trusting him in our difficult situations.

After I rededicated my life to God and learned more about love, I desired peace. I began keeping a peace journal, which I realized later had become a "faith journal" instead. I already believed in God, but my faith was about to be tested. I had to choose if I was going to stand firm on my foundation of Jesus or stumble and fall.

Faith beckons us to take action. We choose to stand firm on our faith in the face of adversity because we know and love the One who called us. We know who we put our faith in. We know who we put our trust in, and we know he loves us and will take care of us.

The balance between having faith and acting on our faith can be compared to having a relationship or a friendship with someone. A person can love the other and build the relationship by spending time with the other person, but at the same time never meet their needs or address their heart's desires. This person can say they love the other until they are blue in the face, but until they demonstrate love towards the other person, it's pointless.

Likewise, if someone has the works, where they do all they can do for the other person and tend to their every need and desire but they lack a loving relationship, then it is equally pointless.

Every relationship has this balance of spending time together and putting the effort in to maintain the relationship. This is shown to us in James 2:14–18 (ESV), "What good is it, my brothers, if someone says he has faith but does not have works? Can that faith save him? If a brother or sister is poorly clothed and lacking in daily food, and one of you says to them, 'Go in peace, be warmed and filled,' without giving them the things needed for the body, what good is that? So also faith by itself, if it does not have works, is dead. But someone will say, 'You have faith and I have works.' Show me your faith apart from your works, and I will show you my faith by my works."

A person cannot be saved by works alone.

In the same way, we are still human and still can stumble and fall. Proverbs 24:16 (ESV) says, "For the righteous falls seven times and rises again, but the wicked stumble in times of calamity." A righteous person will get back up again. He or she will return to the Lord and repent from sins and will receive grace and forgiveness.

Grace is powerful. The Bible repeatedly refers to this special term, "grace." What is the difference between grace, mercy, and judgment? Cathleen Falsani shares it in this way, "Justice is getting what you deserve. Mercy is not getting what you deserve. And grace is getting what you absolutely don't deserve . . . benign good will. Unprovoked compassion. The unearnable gift."[ix]

We cannot earn grace; it is a *gift* from God. The Bible adds in Ephesians 2:8–9 (NIV), "For it is by grace you have been saved, through faith—and this is not from yourselves, it is the gift of God— not by works, so that no one can boast."

God gave us the best present ever, this special gift of grace.

Think back to a time when someone gave you a gift that meant a great deal to you. Likely, it was special because the giver had taken the time to know you and chose this specific gift for you, knowing that you wanted it. The giver was probably someone close to you, who knew you very well.

While I was in college, I was in and out of hospitals for several years with a couple of severe allergies, infections in my ear, and digestive trouble. Thankfully, we found solutions for everything, and I returned to a healthy life. During one of my hospital stays, my mom found a small bunny rabbit with magnetic feet. She clipped it on the side of the hospital bed and told me that even though she could not be there all the time, I could look at the rabbit and remember she was thinking of me and there for me.

At the time I did not find it as special. I was a "grown" woman with a stuffed animal hanging at my bedside. But deep down, I knew it was a special gift from my mom. When I was young and had the flu or another illness, my mom was there for me. She served me lemon-lime soda, chicken noodle soup, and made sure I took the correct medicine to help me get well again.

Years later, I still have that little rabbit hanging off a cabinet in my room. It reminds me of my mom, even though we are miles apart. Now I do not find it so silly. Now I see it as a special gift given out of love during a time of my life when I was far from God and needed some love.

God offers the gift of grace in a similar way. God knows you well. He knows when you fall short, and he knows your heart. Amazingly, he still chose to offer this gift of grace at the cost of the life of his only Son, who never sinned.

After we accept the Lord, he does the unfathomable. He wipes the record of our sins away. He gives us the precious gift of redemption. We are all saved by grace as a gift from God. We have been redeemed. The Lord wiped away our sins and chooses not to remember them any longer. Acts 22:16 (ESV) tells us this, "And now why do you wait? Rise and be baptized and wash away your sins, calling on his name." And Hebrews 8:12 (ESV) adds, "For I will be merciful toward their iniquities, and I will remember their sins no more."

Once I dreamed that I was standing before the Lord on judgment day. He had a great book before him, and as my sins were being read out of this book, a crowd of angels shouted, "Covered by the blood!" over the Lord's voice. Every sin was drowned out by the cheers of the angels that my sin was indeed covered by the blood shed by Jesus. I could not hear a single word that was read except that it was covered by the blood.

Covered by the blood. A high price was paid to cover sin. Jesus died for them all. Every past, future, and present sin, he covers under a blanket of grace as we repent and ask for forgiveness. The best part is that three days after Jesus died, he rose again. Because he rose again, we have the ability to believe the resurrection happened it and, therefore, receive eternal life in Heaven with our Lord.

What an amazing gift! This is the best gift we could be given. Let us not waste the gift, as Paul warns in Romans 6:1–11 (AMP):[x]

What shall we say [to all this]? Should we continue in sin and practice sin as a habit so that [God's gift of] grace may increase and overflow? Certainly not! How can we, the very ones who died to sin, continue to live in it any longer? Or are you ignorant of the fact that all of us who have been baptized into Christ Jesus were baptized into His death? We have therefore been buried with Him through baptism into death, so that just as Christ was raised from the dead through the glory and power of the Father, we too might walk habitually in newness of life [abandoning our old ways]. For if we have become one with Him [permanently united] in the likeness of His death, we will also certainly be [one with Him and share fully] in the likeness of His resurrection. We know that our old self [our human nature without the Holy Spirit] was nailed to the cross with Him, in order that our body of sin might be done away with, so that we would no longer be slaves to sin. For the person who has died [with Christ] has been freed from [the power of] sin.

Now if we have died with Christ, we believe that we will also live [together] with Him, because we know [the self-evident truth] that Christ, having been raised from the dead, will never die again; death no longer has power over Him. For the death that He died, He died to sin [ending its power and paying the sinner's debt] once and for all; and the life that He lives, He lives to [glorify] God [in unbroken fellowship with Him]. Even so, consider yourselves to be dead to sin [and your relationship to it broken], but alive to God [in unbroken fellowship with Him] in Christ Jesus.

Jesus gave his life so we could have a relationship with the Father. We should take him as seriously as he takes us. Choose to follow God and his will. Remember that he is our loving Father, who only wants what is best for us.

"For what does it profit a man to gain the whole world and forfeit his soul?" (Mark 8:36, ESV). You can chase after the things of this life and still never gain all that your heart desires, or you can trust in God and his ways, and he will take care of you. You might never receive everything you desire, but he will walk with you through every situation you face.

The commandments found in the Bible were given in love. Some of the most well-known commands of God are the Ten Commandments found in Exodus 20:1–17 and the two greatest commandments found in Deuteronomy 6:5. However, did you know the word "commandment" is in the Bible 237 times?[xi] That is a lot of commandments! Did you know that the only one who fulfilled the entirety of the law and the commandments was Jesus?

The law, itself, is not love. If we turn to religion over a relationship with Jesus, then we will move further and further away from the Lord. The commandments are there for our aid. They are there to show us right from wrong, but on our own we will never fulfill the commandments. Jesus said in Matthew 5:21–22 (NLT[xii]), "You have heard that our ancestors were told, 'You must not murder. If you commit murder, you are subject to judgment.' But I say, if you are even angry with someone, you are subject to judgment! If you call someone an idiot, you are in danger of being brought before the court. And if you curse someone, you are in danger of the fires of hell."

Wow. That is a strong warning! Thank the Lord for grace that covers us when we mess up.

If we become tempted to believe that we are the only ones who struggle with keeping all the commandments, then we need to take a look at Paul. Paul wrote several of the books in the New Testament, and he, too, struggled with this. Romans 7:7,16–25 (NIV), which he wrote, says, "What shall we say, then? Is the law sinful? Certainly not! Nevertheless, I would not have known what sin was had it not been for the law. For I would not have known what coveting really was if the law had not said, 'You shall not covet.' I do not understand what I do. For what I want to do I do not do, but what I hate I do. And if I do what I do not want to do, I agree that the law is good. As it is, it is no longer I myself who do it, but it is sin living in me. For I know that good itself does not dwell in me, that is, in my sinful nature. For I have the desire to do what is good, but I cannot carry it out. For I do not do the good I want to do, but the evil I do not want to do—this I keep on doing. Now if I do what I do not want to do, it is no longer I who do it, but it is sin living in me that does it.

"So I find this law at work: Although I want to do good, evil is right there with me. For in my inner being I delight in God's law; but I see another law at work in me, waging war against the law of my mind and making me a prisoner of the law of sin at work within me. What a wretched man I am! Who will rescue me from this body that is subject to death? Thanks be to God, who delivers me through Jesus Christ our Lord!"

This is the battle between our flesh and Spirit. The Holy Spirit shows us the right way and reminds us of the commandments to help us choose the way of the Lord. On the other hand if we are not careful, our fleshly desires can make a pretty convincing argument and lead us astray. As Paul says, "Thanks be to God, who delivers me through Jesus Christ our Lord!"

Persevere. Keep going and moving onward. Ask for forgiveness when you need to, and trust God with the rest. He will guide you. Remember that grace covers sin! Accept that God loves you and that he will forgive when you fail, but attempt to obey him and follow his Word. We all want to finish strong and make it to the end of our life with Jesus.

During junior high and high school, I was involved in cross-country running. We ran two-mile races in junior high and three-mile races in high school. At the end of every race, when the finish line came into view, the runners activated a reserved kick of speed. This was my favorite part of the race. Mostly because it was almost over, but also because that last kick was the final amount of energy left. It used everything you had. Some runners lost their spot in the last few yards of the race.

I won a race during high school, and I had been behind nearly the entire three miles. My coach found me during the second mile, the hardest mile, and she encouraged me by sharing that the runner in view ahead of me was in first place.

I have not forgotten that because it gave me hope. I realized I had a chance to win a race, so I stayed close—close enough that I knew my end kick could launch me into first place. Again, my coach found me in the third mile, just before the finish line was in sight. She leaned in and whispered so that the other girl did not know how close I was. She told me that I was almost at the end, and it was time to go, now or never. Then as I activated the last bit of energy I had to race ahead, she shouted, "Go Brooke, Go!"

And I ran like I never had before. You see, when my coach told me to run, it was earlier than I had ever started a final kick. I had to hold out longer and faster than ever before. Just when I started to become doubtful and discouraged, I saw my dad at the top of the hill and knew I was going to do it for him. It was the first race, and one of the only races, I ever won.

Most fans and family watch the beginning of the race, and they are there for the end to cheer you on. But, a great coach finds the hardest places, the steepest hills, and plants himself or herself there to encourage the team members at their weakest moments. My coach would some-times even run with us a few paces to push us along.

The Lord is a great coach. He stands at the hardest places and gives you encouragement. He runs with you, right by your side, cheering you on.

He wants to see you finish well, and he knows that throughout the whole race of life, you would need someone to be there for you. That is why we have the Holy Spirit to help us on our hardest days. That is why we have the Word of God to turn to and strengthen us. And, that is why the Father stands at the end of our race, ready to celebrate victory with us. God knows we cannot do it alone, and he wants to see us finish well. He wants us to have the strength for that final kick at the end of our race so that we, too, can finish well.

Review Questions:

- Think about where you are with Christ right now. Have you ac-cepted him as Lord of your life?
- What is the starting place of faith?

Scripture memory verse:

Ephesians 4:22-24 (ESV)

"Put off your old self, which belongs to your former manner of life and is corrupt through deceitful desires, and to be renewed in the spirit of your minds, and to put on the new self, created after the likeness of God in true righteousness and holiness."

Challenge:

Write out the Romans Road and put it in a place you will see it.

CHAPTER 5

Faith: As We Grow

A small town called Wilmore, Kentucky held one of the largest revivals this nation has witnessed in my lifetime. A private, Christian university called Asbury University suddenly burst at the seams with thousands of people. So many people came to the revival that roads were backed up and parking was nearly impossible. I was blessed to be able to attend the 2023 Asbury Revival.

Throughout the few weeks it lasted, people flocked there from across the nation and around the world. I witnessed people who had a deep hunger for God and his Word. Many people came to seek his presence in their lives and feel his touch. Young people were laying their lives down to pick up the cross.

The room I was in held people of all ages and languages coming together to worship the Lord and seeking for him to work in their lives. Many of the people present went to the altar during the quiet prayer time. My prayer is that the decisions made for Christ throughout the revival took root and are flourishing.

A lot of people came and went in the chapel while I was there. I sat behind the sweetest family for quite a while. Their little toddler was very hungry! The family would hold up a food item, and she would shake her head no until they picked the food she wanted.

This reminded me of what was taking place at Asbury. People were saying, "No, the world is not it. The world is not what I want." They had a hunger and a desire for Jesus instead!

If you long to have a deeper craving for the Lord and know him more, ask him to help you grow in desire for him. May we, too, dive into a greater hunger for the Lord in our lives and say no to the "worldly food" we should not desire.

When I knew it was time for me to leave Asbury, I asked the Lord why. He answered, "Because you are full." Full indeed. Filled with the love of the Lord and for his people after sitting in God's presence. I was ready to go out and share it.

May this hunger to know and experience God more continue to nurture in the hearts of his people. Now that many from the Asbury revival have accepted Jesus as their Savior, they may be wondering what is next. Like you, they wonder how the decisions they made for Christ could take root and flourish. They have taken the first step, one of faith, and will now begin their journey of growing in the Lord and following his leading.

Another way to look at growing in faith is to see it as learning to trust God more. We need to remember that God loves us and wants what is best for us, even if this does not look like what we think is best for us. So, we must trust him, even though it is hard. But how can we trust God if we do not know his voice's gentle leading?

Jesus is the good shepherd who guides us, and we need to hear him in order to follow him. John 10:1–5 (ESV) says, "Truly, truly, I say to you, he who does not enter the sheepfold by the door but climbs in by another way, that man is a thief and a robber. But he who enters by the door is the shepherd of the sheep. To him the gatekeeper opens. The sheep hear his voice, and he calls his own sheep by name and leads them out. When he has brought out all his own, he goes before them, and the sheep follow him, for they know his voice. A stranger they will not follow, but they will flee from him, for they do not know the voice of strangers."

For many years I could not understand how to hear the Lord's voice correctly, and I was so afraid of getting it wrong that I could not begin to figure out how to get it right. The primary way that God speaks to his people is through their reading the Holy Bible. Yes, that's it. Not some big ceremony or special prayer, but by prayerfully and intentionally reading the Word of God.

It is like when we talked about inviting a friend over and not spending time with that friend. The more you spend time with someone, the more you get to know what the person likes and dislikes. The scriptures point out exactly what God's thoughts are on sin, his people, and how to live a righteous life.

The Lord can also speak to us through the Holy Spirit. We must be in the Word to confirm that the voice we hear is something that the Lord would say. First John 4:1 (ESV) says, "Beloved, do not believe every spirit, but test the spirits to see whether they are from God, for many false prophets have gone out into the world."

Test and make sure that what you hear lines up with scripture.

Soon after I rededicated my life to the Lord in college, I was very focused on finding my calling. I was dedicated to finding exactly what God had planned for me to do in this life, and I sought an answer from the Holy Spirit about it. However, the direction did not come right away. In fact, it was almost ten years after college when I found out what my calling was, and it was a simple one at that. I was to share the message of Jesus with everyone I could, using the gifts he has given me. And guess what? That is your calling too. If you are a follower of Jesus, then that is your mission in life.

In the last moments Jesus spent with his disciples before ascending to Heaven, he gave them the Great Commission. This was after he rose from the grave and had met with them several times. We find his Great Commission in Matthew 28:16–20 (ESV), "Now the eleven disciples went to Galilee, to the mountain to which Jesus had directed them. And when they saw him they worshiped him, but some doubted. And Jesus came and said to them, 'All authority in heaven and on earth has been given to me. Go therefore and make disciples of all nations, baptizing them in the name of the Father and of the Son and of the Holy Spirit, teaching them to observe all that I have commanded you. And behold, I am with you always, to the end of the age.'"

This is our mission as believers. Living out this mission will look different from person to person, based on where we live and how we use the gifts we have received. The Holy Spirit can lead someone to go to a certain place or do a specific type of work to share the gospel, but at the foundation, all believers receive the same calling. So, if you were like me and did not know exactly what God wants you to do for the rest of your life, rest in knowing that as you wait for his answer, you are called to be committed to serving him and sharing him with others.

My Papaw found his calling late in life. Even when he was in college, he knew he was called into ministry, but not to be a pastor. One day, he finally found his calling when a campground needed a cook for their teen camp. Without any prior training in food service, my grandparents agreed to help out in the kitchen that year. One thing led to another and eventually my grandparents became the camp cooks. They also ended up cooking at several other campgrounds with mission organizations that led them all across the United States. They had a heart for the people and knew how to serve food in love. Now, folks across the nation and even across the world call them Mom and Dad because of the love they showed. They truly found their calling.

When we put our faith in God, he gives us his peace. Remember my peace journal that became a faith journal? I realized that the more I sought God's peace, the more I was growing in trusting him and putting my faith in him.

I want to encourage you to choose to have faith over choosing to be crippled in fear. Faith in God can do something about the situation, and even if God does not change the situation, he promises to walk through it with you. Choosing to go through a situation without God will make it worse and a lonely journey. Plant your feet firmly on the foundation of Jesus so that when the storms blow, you will not be knocked over. When the storms, or trials of life come, turn to Jesus. Read the Word, pray, and trust him to help you along the way and thusly you will have planted your feet firmly on the foundation of Jesus.

My favorite Bible portion to turn to during my multiple hospital visits was the book of Job. Job was a blameless and upright man whom God blessed. The devil thought that if Job's family, livelihood, and health were removed, Job would turn against God.

God knew that Job would stand the test, so he allowed the devil to test Job. Job became sorrowful as he had lost everything except the Lord, but he knew that he was not being punished for sinning against God. In fact, he brazenly told God that! Through all of this, Job never lost his faith in God, and in the end of the story, the Lord rewarded him mightily. Job planted his feet on the Lord and dug in deep when life became its hardest.

Like Job, we can have faith while in our own circumstances. A few years ago, a minister named Noel Bates shared at a camp service I attended. He shared about having faith through negative circumstances in our lives. He made four powerful points about this. Noel shared with us that first, faith sometimes changes our circumstances. Second, faith sometimes does not change our circumstances. Next, faith never judges or questions God. And finally, faith always leads to ultimate victory.[xiii]

Faith in God will sometimes change our circumstances. I used to live a little over two hours away from the campground I grew up attending with my grandparents, and I would volunteer there on the weekends I had off of work. I had a cheap car that held up well under the many miles. Yet, the real reason that I made it back and forth safely every time was that I always prayed that the Lord would watch over me and help me not to have any car trouble. I knew I could trust God with my car, and he would take care of me because I gave the situation to him. I have had a few miracles take place with the cars I have had.

The first miracle was the day the engine died in my car. I was about forty minutes into the drive, and my car started acting unusual. I pulled off on the side of the road. I had stopped at the outskirts of a town I was passing through. Then, I turned the car off, and to my surprise, it would not turn back on. I had been on this route many times before, and I knew I would only pass only one car repair place on the trip. My car had stopped less than one hundred feet away from it.

I walked to the shop, and the owners towed my car to the shop for free. They allowed me to wait in the air-conditioned lobby until my dad came from almost an hour and a half away to pick me up. They informed me of the engine's situation and also let my car sit at their shop for a week until we could transport it to the junkyard. Wow, only God!

The next miracle was with my second car. I had moved to a different city by this point and was on my way home from work. I had already run several errands in the city where I worked before heading home on the nearby interstate instead of my usual highway route. I had driven for approximately thirty minutes before my car had started acting funny. I continued for another ten minutes.

My car began wobbling more, and I remember the Holy Spirit whisper to me that, "Today would not be a bad day for a flat tire. You have plenty of time and need oil change. Plus, that one in the back has been getting flatter recently."

Sadly, instead of responding with a faith-filled "yes," I said, "No, I will not stop" rather foolishly instead. As soon as I rebelliously thought those words, *pop!* My tire flattened. Ugh, I should have listened. I apologized to the Lord quickly and pulled over the study the tire that I assumed had flattened.

To my surprise it looked fine. I looked at the front and discovered the culprit. There it was—completely flat with the rim resting on the ground. A few years before this, I had a flat front tire that completely lunged my entire car with each wheel rotation.

That memory frightened me as I studied my situation. I was also concerned that I may not be able to drive anywhere without further, costly damage to the rim. I looked at the road ahead and amazingly saw a sign for an auto repair shop! My car was only about a mile away. So, I turned my flashers on, drove slowly on the shoulder, and amazingly, I was no longer afraid. God had it! So, I went for it! The tire had a small amount of air in it, but the traction of the tire with the asphalt created a burning odor.

However, I prayed and asked God to prevent damage to the rim. I hoped I would avoid needing the rim repaired. After a slow mile, I made it! I started praising the Lord and shouting of God's goodness. I checked my car into the shop. Not only did they find that the rim had no damage, but also, they had enough time to replace both drivers' side tires and complete an oil change. Praise the Lord!

Sometimes faith will not change our circumstances. Many years ago, I was talking with a very godly man. We had several similarities and decided to start dating. I was very excited and felt that the Lord had put us together. I had received what I believed to confirmation that this was the relationship for me.

When the relationship ended sooner than I expected, I could not understand why. I felt that the Lord had brought me into a relationship with this man, and I could not understand what happened. Meanwhile, this mighty man of faith felt as though God told him that the relationship needed to end.

I cried to the Lord in my grief and prayed for the situation to change. I was broken and didn't understand. At that time, I realized that I had to choose: Would I trust God even though this situation did not end like I had hoped, or would I wallow in sadness and wish for things to be different?

At first, I wanted to know why God had told him one thing and me another. Some wise and kind friends told me that if God wanted it to happen, it would happen, and if not, then I was still to trust God, even if it did not work out. I believe that God was showing me that that relationship lasted exactly as long as it was supposed to.

No amount of faith, praying, fasting, or crying out to the Lord changed my circumstance. Instead, it changed me. I realized that I had not had a lack of faith in God like I had been struggling with. I had not lost faith in God. I believed what I had thought I heard the Lord say. But when the relationship came to an end, I had a hard time believing it at first. Over time, I learned to instead cling to the promises of God and trust him. I turned to promises that are found in scripture like, "I will never leave you nor forsake you" (Hebrews 13:5, ESV) and "Trust in the Lord with all your heart, and do not lean on your own understanding. In all your ways acknowledge him, and he will make straight your paths" (Proverbs 3:5–6 ESV). I tested them, clung to them, and found them true. We can count on the Word of God every time.

God used this difficult situation to teach me about growing in faith more than any other situation I had faced before. I had to theoretically set an anchor down to attach myself to Jesus and trust God even when my flesh did not understand. The Lord is faithful, and he led me through the situation and taught me a lesson that influenced my understanding of faith. Due to that, I can look back in understanding and be thankful for the lessons the Lord taught me. Sometimes, faith in God will not change our circumstances but God will walk through them with us.

The next two attributes of faith can be found in the stories of two miracle men I knew. One was healed this side of Heaven; the other was healed in Heaven. These men were in the hospital the same week. Both had faith that can move mountains. The first miracle man is a family member of mine, a cousin, who is a walking medical miracle. Time and time again, he has proven the doctor's timeline for his life to be wrong. He has survived more than most people I know and leads a life devoted to the Lord. He recently became kidney transplant recipient as a young adult.

Faith never judges or questions God. My cousin shows this well. He never complains. He has been through many procedures and surgeries, ones that are painful for the strongest of us, and he does not complain. He does not ask God why he was born that way or why he has to struggle to survive more than most. He does not tell God that he was wrong to make him that way. Instead, he has the biggest heart after God and love for his neighbor.

Due to this, greater glory is given to God through his testimony. My cousin's story has touched many lives, and he has many people regularly praying for him. He has been healed this side of Heaven multiple times.

Faith always leads to ultimate victory. The other miracle man is a lot like my cousin. He was the oldest living double-transplant survivor and outlasted what was presumed to be medically possible. He was healed many times this side of Heaven. He too could have complained about many things, but instead, he chose to glorify God through them. He started a kids' club for his neighborhood because one little boy came to his doorstep to ask for a cup of water. The ministry has grown to over one hundred kids and their families being fed by a team of volunteers. It also started serving the homeless community recently.

My friend's motto was "pray big" and boy did he! God showed up in mighty ways in his life, and he was always filled with the joy of the Lord. My friend loved to make people laugh! That kids club is now thriving and the children are learning to love their neighbors well.

God knew that this miracle man's work was done, and so God called him home. My cousin went home to his house from the hospital, and my friend went home to Heaven that same week. My friend left this earth with a huge smile on his face, for he was getting ready to see Jesus face to face! He won the victory and finished his race well.

May we, too, cling to God no matter what comes and finish our races well.

Believers are still learning until they day they are called home. Sometimes, we go to God first at the first sign of trouble. While at other times, we try to handle things on our own first. It can take time for us to realize we need to go to the Lord first.

At times we will mess up. But, to talk about faith, we must also talk about grace. Faith and grace go hand in hand. Since we love God as our Father and we attempt to refrain from sinning, we can go before him when we do sin. He offers grace and forgiveness when we come to him with a repentant heart.

We have already learned a lot about grace in this book, but there is so much more to it. The Bible is full of stories and teachings of grace. One of the most well know parables is the Parable of the Prodigal Son found in Luke 15:11–32. A father had two sons. One of the sons asked for the inheritance he would normally receive after the parents had passed. Instead of using the funds wisely, he left his home and spent all of his money on frivolous things. Once the money was gone, a famine struck, and he sought a job feeding a farmer's pigs. Eventually he came to his senses and realized that his father's own servants were fed better than he was eating. At last, he returned to his father's house with the plan to become a servant in his father's house. On the son's journey home, the father saw him coming from a distance and ran to him. The father did not acknowledge the son's plea to become a servant, but instead restored the son to his former status in the household.

The older son was out in a field when he saw the commotion, and he became angry when he learned that the foolish son had been restored in the household. The father went to the older son and asked him to come inside to celebrate. The older son spoke to the father about how upset he was since he had never turned from serving the father. The father's response is found in Luke 15:31–32 (ESV), "And he said to him, 'Son, you are always with me, and all that is mine is yours. It was fitting to celebrate and be glad, for this your brother was dead, and is alive; he was lost, and is found.'"

This is many of our own stories. We, too, were wandering far from God and took advantage of what he gave us, and when the sinful lifestyle caught up with us one day, we decided to return to the Father, just like the prodigal son. Instead of being met with anger and being cast out, we found that the Lord restored us as a child and celebrated our return.

Romans 3:23–25 (ESV) tells us, "For all have sinned and fall short of the glory of God, and are justified by his grace as a gift, through the redemption that is in Christ Jesus, whom God put forward as a propitiation by his blood, to be received by faith."

We are all guilty of sin, but by grace, we have been redeemed. When I think of my own relationship with the Father, the first word that comes to my mind is "redeemed." I was redeemed from my life of sin by the grace of God.

When we accept Jesus into our lives, we are given grace. Romans 4:16 (ESV) show us, "That is why it depends on faith, in order that the promise may rest on grace and be guaranteed to all his offspring."

Romans 5:2 (ESV) add, "Through him, we have also obtained access by faith into this grace in which we stand."

Due to Jesus coming to earth, dying on the cross, and rising again, the way to Heaven was opened up for those that believe, and we are given grace that covers all our sins. Grace is a gift, "But the free gift is not like the trespass. For if many died through [Adam's] trespass, much more have the grace of God and the free gift by the grace of that one man Jesus Christ abounded for many" (Romans 5:15, ESV).

"What does grace look like? Devine grace is the undeserved favor of a superior bestowed on an inferior."[xiv] Grace is a free gift given to all who believe in Jesus. Free. No strings attached. There is no, "I gave you this so you must do this."

Grace is like taking a dirty dish and washing it. The dish can be used again and dirtied, but it will need to be cleaned again. After some time, the dish will be stained by its years of being dirtied.

My Memaw has a case of fine dishes with beautiful decorations adorning them. We have never eaten off of these dishes, and we probably never will. These dishes are richly engraved and set apart due to their beauty. They are not stained with food particles from many years of wear and tear, even though they are years older than the other dishes. Why? It's because they have rarely been used for food.

Our lives are like this. We can be continually washed and wiped clean after sin, but the sin-stains ultimately touch our lives. Eventually, even if we continually go before the Lord and ask him to cleanse us when we mess up, the consequences of our actions can still affect us down the road. God still clean us over and over, but it is better to not sin than to willingly sin and rely on grace to clean us up again and again.

As believers, we are set apart like the dishes were. Galatians 1:15 (ESV) says, "he who had set me apart before I was born, and who called me by his grace."

Perhaps we did not start as dishes in the fine China cabinet. Maybe we were found at a yard sale and our potential was recognized. We were bought for a certain price and taken home and washed up. After being cleaned, we were set apart and placed in the China cabinet for all to see. Nowadays, a fine China cabinet is not common and many people do not see the same beauty in the dishes as the purchaser once did. A visitor might not have the same feeling towards the dishes as the purchaser does. The visitor might share that the dishes should be sold or discarded. They might point out the broken pieces or treat them poorly, but the purchaser knows that they were bought by a price and takes care in how they handle them.

The world is like the visitor. Often, they are unable to see the value within the believer. They may not see their worth, like the visitor could not see the cost and time spent behind the dishes. The visitors, like the world, will point out the flaws and broken pieces and even cause the breaking themselves sometimes, but this does not change how the Lord sees us. He bought us with a price and washed us clean. By his grace we are saved, and the worldly cannot understand it. But every once in a while, they will see the value of knowing Christ and turn to the Lord themselves.

A beautiful dish can be found anywhere. It might be so covered in dust, dirt, or food stains so that no one could think that it would be valuable, but God knows its worth. Collectors will add an item to their collection no matter how dirty the item is, because they know its value. God knows our value, and those cleaned, yet food-stained plates? They are found right beside the others that were rarely used for food in the curio cabinet. The purchaser knew how valuable they were all along; they just needed to be cleaned first.

Review Questions:

- What are the four outcomes of having faith during our circumstances?
- How was the younger son shown grace in the parable of the Prodigal Son?

Scripture memory verse:

Romans 5:15, ESV

"But the free gift is not like the trespass. For if many died through one man's trespass, much more have the grace of God and the free gift by the grace of that one man Jesus Christ abounded for many."

Challenge:

Take some time to pray about where God is calling and leading you. What is he laying on your heart?

CHAPTER 6

Faith: Where We Are Heading

Two opposing teams stand on either side of a thin line. Both forces are evenly matched with the same number of people on either side as they battle back and forth to win. The red team advances and is on the offense, and then a shift occurs when the goalie catches the soccer ball and punts it back into the blue team's corner. The blue team retreats and reassembles as the ball bounces out of bounds.

Suddenly, there is a substitute. A player from the red team exits while another one enters the field. To the blue team's dismay, the new player for the red team is the best in the region. This player is well known for scoring countless goals, and the blue team's faces become crestfallen. Visible discouragement spreads like a wave from the blue team's player to player. The game is practically lost before it is over.

Now picture this mighty soccer player as a fierce warrior in a battlefield instead. He is strong and tactical, knowing his strength comes solely from the Lord. "How does he know his strength comes solely from the Lord," you may ask? This man knows he started at the bottom of a hierarchy and was low on the pecking order and the Lord pulled him out of the pit. At the beginning of his story, we learn that this man's mother was a prostitute, and his stepsiblings were not willing to share in their father's inheritance with him. Ultimately, his brothers drove him out of the house. Then, he went to live with some of the roughest folks around.

Great introduction for a mighty man of faith, right? He was the son of a prostitute with no inheritance and was an outcast in his own family, but God did not leave him there. God saw his potential to lead his people and others began to as well. He became like that soccer player, whose presence on the field turned the other team to dismay.

Who is this man? His name is Jephthah, and his story is found in Judges 11 and 12. Jephthah is also listed in Hebrews 11, which is often referred to as the "Hall of Faith" chapter. "And what more shall I say? For time would fail me to tell of Gideon, Barak, Samson, Jephthah, of David and Samuel and the prophets—who through faith conquered kingdoms, enforced justice, obtained promises, stopped the mouths of lions, quenched the power of fire, escaped the edge of the sword, were made strong out of weakness, became mighty in war, put foreign armies to flight" (Hebrews 11:32–34, ESV).

When I first read this passage, I knew of the others listed. I had heard of Gideon, Barak, Samson, David, and Samuel, but who was this Jephthah? How did he become known as a mighty warrior (Judges 11:1, ESV)?

We find this story in Judges 11:5–9 (ESV), "And when the Ammonites made war against Israel, the elders of Gilead went to bring Jephthah from the land of Tob. And they said to Jephthah, 'Come and be our leader, that we may fight against the Ammonites.' But Jephthah said to the elders of Gilead, 'Did you not hate me and drive me out of my father's house? Why have you come to me now when you are in distress?' And the elders of Gilead said to Jephthah, 'That is why we have turned to you now, that you may go with us and fight against the Ammonites and be our head over all the inhabitants of Gilead.' Jephthah said to the elders of Gilead, 'If you bring me home again to fight against the Ammonites, and the Lord gives them over to me, I will be your head.'"

Jephthah was "made strong out of weakness, became mighty in war, put foreign armies to flight" as referenced in Hebrews 11:34, but he did not know the law and the Lord as well as he thought he did. When he exchanged words with the Ammonites, he had some of Israel's and the Ammonites' history incorrect. He also made a tragic vow that was similar to the Ammonites' way of worshipping their own god. We learn of this tragic vow in Judges 11:29–32 (NIV), "Then the Spirit of the Lord came on Jephthah. He crossed Gilead and Manasseh, passed through Mizpah of Gilead, and from there he advanced against the Ammonites. And Jephthah made a vow to the Lord; 'If you give the Ammonites into my hands, whatever comes out of the door of my house to meet me when I return in triumph from the Ammonites will be the Lord's, and I will sacrifice it as a burnt offering. Then Jephthah went over to fight the Ammonites, and the Lord gave them into his hands."

The result of the tragic vow is found in verses 34–36 (NIV), "When Jephthah returned to his home in Mizpah, who should come out to meet him but his daughter, dancing to the sound of the timbrels! She was an only child. Except for her he had neither son nor daughter. When he saw her, he tore his clothes and cried, 'Oh no, my daughter! You have brought me down and I am devastated. I have made a vow to the Lord that I cannot break.' 'My father,' she replied, 'you have given your word to the Lord. Do to me just as you promised, now that the Lord has avenged you of your enemies, the Ammonites.'"

This story breaks my heart. Why would Jephthah vow this? Why would he sacrifice his daughter? Why did the Lord not stop him?

I did not have the answer, so I went to my study Bible and the notes. It said, "The coming of the Spirit of the Lord upon Jephthah (i.e., his empowerment) should have been the guarantee of victory, but his vow will undermine everything. Jephthah's vow is manipulative, promising a burnt offering in exchange for victory. It is also rash in its qualification: 'whatever comes out of the door of my house to meet me.' Given the arrangement of homes with courtyards that housed domesticated animals, Jephthah may have intended that one of these animals be encountered first upon his return home. Nevertheless, it was a distinct possibility that it would be a human being.

"This is ironic because Jephthah had delivered the Israelites from the Ammonites, who sacrificed their children to Molek, yet Jephthah sacrifices his daughter to the Lord, who does not accept human sacrifice. Unfortunately, other Israelites offered human sacrifices too (2 Kings 16:3; 21:6; Ezekiel 20:25–26, 31). Jephthah's ignorance of the law is compounded: he could have redeemed his daughter (Leviticus 27:1–8). While a vow was not to be broken (Numbers 30:2; Deuteronomy 23:21–23), God had provided the means for redemption of vows. Jephthah was apparently ignorant of this."[xv]

Jephthah was the one who made the vow based on whether or not he would succeed, the Lord did not tell him to do so. Why did the Lord not stop him? Well, the Lord had also worked a way of escape from this vow into the law, but Jephthah was not well learned of the law. Instead of turning to the scriptures and learning more about God beforehand, Jephthah became leader of a nation while being not very familiar with the law of the nation, and he sacrificed his daughter to God, who does not delight in human sacrifice. His faith was in God, but he did not know the word of the Lord very well and, unfortunately, it came back against him through his own words. This is a good example of why it is so important to be reading the Word to know God for ourselves and to mind our words.

We should not barter with God, saying if he gives us this, then we will do this or that. God wants our whole heart, not for us to bargain with him. Before I rededicated my life to God, I would be in my room looking for an item. Apparently, it was something I strongly believed I needed because I would say, *Lord I know I don't talk to you much but if you could help me find this, then I will do a better job of following you.*

Low and behold, I would find the item, but my life would continue just as it had before. I would thank him and truly meant it, but my promise fell short every time. God does not want our vows and promises, he wants us to give him our whole heart and decide to follow him all of our days. He knows our hearts and whether or not our words will hold true.

Matthew 5:33-37 (NIV) tells us of this, "Again, you have heard that it was said to the people long ago, 'Do not break your oath, but fulfill to the Lord the vows you have made.' But I tell you, do not swear an oath at all: either by heaven, for it is God's throne; or by the earth, for it is his footstool; or by Jerusalem, for it is the city of the Great King. And do not swear by your head, for you cannot make even one hair white or black. All you need to say is simply 'Yes' or 'No'; anything beyond this comes from the evil one."

Do not make these promises you cannot keep. The only one who can keep his promises is God. God keeps the promises he makes. If you say yes to something, try to fulfill it. If you say no, then do not do what you said you would not. God is still a God of grace and mercy, but we should not put ourselves in "I promise" situations.

Jesus is the ultimate example of perfect faith. He is fully God and fully man, but he also demonstrated the relationship we can have with the Father. One way Jesus taught us about faith is by telling us to look to the Father for our needs and desires. Before he performed miracles, Jesus acknowledged the Father. Every miracle Jesus did was through faith in the Father. John 11:1-57 contains the story of Lazarus being raised from the dead. John 11:41–42 (ESV) says, "So they took away the stone. And Jesus lifted up his eyes and said, 'Father, I thank you that you have heard me. I knew that you always hear me, but I said this on account of the people standing around, that they may believe that you sent me.'"

Jesus had already prayed to the Father for the life of Lazarus and had faith that the Father would raise Lazarus from the dead. He trusted the Father and had faith that the Father would do what he said he would do.

God can intertwine purpose in our own hard things, as we trust him through it all. Mary and Martha were saddened by their brother dying, but they still trusted God to work it all out in the end. Remember that God can still perform miracles to this day. Trust Him, even when it is difficult.

John 9:1–3 tells of a blind man who was healed, "As he passed by, he saw a man blind from birth. And his disciples asked him, 'Rabbi, who sinned, this man or his parents, that he was born blind?' Jesus answered, 'It was not that this man sinned, or his parents, but that the works of God might be displayed in him.'"

God brought about many miracles in hard situations and used them to lead many people to believe in Jesus.

Perhaps one of the most substantial stories of Jesus' faith in the Father is when Jesus prayed in the Garden of Gethsemane. We find this in Matthew 26:36-39 (ESV), "Then Jesus went with them to a place called Gethsemane, and he said to his disciples, 'Sit here, while I go over there and pray.' And taking with him Peter and the two sons of Zebedee, he began to be sorrowful and troubled. Then he said to them, 'My soul is very sorrowful, even to death; remain here, and watch with me.' And going a little farther he fell on his face and prayed, saying, 'My Father, if it be possible, let this cup pass from me; nevertheless, not as I will, but as you will.'"

Jesus was fully man and fully God. His human nature knew the physical pain he would experience on the cross, and it wanted to say "no." However, Jesus humbled himself to obey the Father's will. Jesus chose to lay down his life to save the world. No one made him do it. Luke 23:46 (ESV) tells us this, "Then Jesus, calling out with a loud voice, said, 'Father, into your hands I commit my spirit!' And having said this he breathed his last."

Jesus knew that unless he died for us, we would never have a chance to experience eternal life. He did it for you and for me.

Obedience to the Father comes from recognizing that he is our loving Father and only wants what is best for us. He cares more about making sure our spiritual health is in the right place than about our physical health. Our physical bodies will one day pass away, but our spirit will live on. We want to be in Heaven. There is no use in being in fantastic physical health but missing the destination of Heaven.

The Bible is full of stories of people who had faith in God, as well as many stories of people like Jephthah who had made mistakes. When

I learned to trust in God and rely on him, I had peace. Some days, the world rages, and I still need the reminder to turn to Jesus and trust him even when it does not make sense.

At its essence, faith is understanding that God is our loving Father and he has great plans for us. Jeremiah 29:11 (ESV) tells us this, "'For I know the plans I have for you,' declares the Lord, 'plans to prosper you and not to harm you, plans to give you hope and a future.'"

Since we have believed that Jesus is God's Son and that Jesus came to earth, died on the cross, and rose again on the third day to offer us eternal life, we can have peace in the storms of life. Without God, we are like the disciples in the boat who were afraid. Jesus was in the boat with them, but they were afraid in the midst of the storm.

This story is found in Mark 4:35-41 (ESV), "On that day, when evening had come, he said to them, 'Let us go across to the other side.' And leaving the crowd, they took him with them in the boat, just as he was. And other boats were with him. And a great windstorm arose, and the waves were breaking into the boat, so that the boat was already filling. But he was in the stern, asleep on the cushion. And they woke him and said to him, 'Teacher, do you not care that we are perishing?' And he awoke and rebuked the wind and said to the sea, 'Peace! Be still!' And the wind ceased, and there was a great calm. He said to them, 'Why are you so afraid? Have you still no faith?' And they were filled with great fear and said to one another, 'Who then is this, that even the wind and the sea obey him?'"

Have you no faith? The disciples walked with Jesus, they saw the miracles, and yet their faith was shaken. I too have had my faith shaken, and I was inspired to write down the times I remembered God coming through for me in the past. I took a full page of my journal and wrote:

"Faith Moments—thankful moments when God showed up"

1. April 17th, 2012- became a Christian.

2. The day God sent an angel to save my life so I didn't fall on the sign right behind me at the lake.
3. My Great Banquet weekend.
4. The time the tarp flew off of the car in front of me and went under my car. I pulled over and dragged it out from underneath with no problems and no wreck!
5. The day my first car's engine died within 100 feet of the only repair place on the trip.
6. The day at camp where we prayed for a sign to minister to others and I "saw" Gail in a vision and then met her in person later.
7. God delivered a second car that was affordable.
8. My baptism.
9. When I got a job at a retail store after I was told I couldn't work there since I left the orientation to go on a mission trip to China.
10. When I got a job at a bank even though I stumbled through my words during the interview.
11. When God gave me a home church when I wasn't searching for it and didn't realize I needed it.
12. When I got a job at camp after applying to at least fifty occupations with no avail.
13. When I got on the last train into China with precious cargo.
14. But God isn't finished yet! And He works miracles! He answers prayers!

Have you created a list yet? What does your list look like? Do you have unbelievable experiences on there like I do? Your list will only make sense to you and God, but place it somewhere so you can turn to it when you start to doubt and feel afraid.

How do we face our fears? First, we need to fear God alone. In the love chapters, we discovered that God is our loving Father, and we are to have a healthy fear and respect for him as we would our parents.

Deuteronomy 6:13 (ESV) says, "It is the Lord your God you shall fear." While Deuteronomy 10:12–13 (ESV) adds, "And now, Israel, what does the Lord your God require of you, but to fear the Lord your God, to walk in all his ways, to love him, to serve the Lord your God with all your heart and with all your soul, and to keep the commandments and statutes of the Lord, which I am commanding you today for your good?"

We are to have a holy reverential fear of the Lord, walk in his ways, love him, serve him, and keep his commands.

Due to the Lord being the one we should have a holy fear of, this means we are to neither fear man nor circumstances. Hebrews 13:5–7 (ESV) tells us we are not to fear man; "Keep your life free from love of money, and be content with what you have, for he has said, 'I will never leave you nor forsake you.' So we can confidently say, 'The Lord is my helper; I will not fear; what can man do to me?' Remember your leaders, those who spoke to you the word of God. Consider the outcome of their way of life, and imitate their faith."

Look for a mentor who points you to God. God alone is our accountability partner, but we can have other believers who come along side us and help teach us about God. Have faith and let God guide you. If your trust is in God, then you too can choose not to fear as the author of Hebrews instructed. Isaiah 41:10 (ESV) adds, "Fear not, for I am with you; be not dismayed, for I am your God; I will strengthen you, I will help you, I will uphold you with my righteous right hand."

Let God hold you up instead of people, because a person will always fail you. God is the only one who never fails.

The phone rings and you experience the dreaded phone call; your family member died soon after an accident. Or you are at the doctors' office and they are scheduling a biopsy to check a growing lump in your underarm. Or you are changing jobs and wondering if this one would be better than the last.

In any of these situations, fear raises its ugly head. What do you do? Sometimes this is a hard place where we just want to give in to fear. But we are still called to trust God. In Mark 5:36 (ESV) Jesus said to Jarius, "Do not fear, only believe."

This call is to us as well as Jarius: "Do not fear, only believe."

The Lord does not want us to worry. In fact, Matthew 6:25–34 (ESV) covers an entire passage about it. "Therefore I tell you, do not be anxious about your life, what you will eat or what you will drink, nor about your body, what you will put on. Is not life more than food, and the body more than clothing? Look at the birds of the air: they neither sow nor reap nor gather into barns, and yet your heavenly Father feeds them. Are you not of more value than they? And which of you by being anxious can add a single hour to his span of life? And why are you anxious about clothing? Consider the lilies of the field, how they grow: they neither toil nor spin, yet I tell you, even Solomon in all his glory was not arrayed like one of these. But if God so clothes the grass of the field, which today is alive and tomorrow is thrown into the oven, will he not much more clothe you, O you of little faith? Therefore do not be anxious, saying, 'What shall we eat?' or 'What shall we drink?' or 'What shall we wear?' For the Gentiles seek after all these things, and your heavenly Father knows that you need them all. But seek first the kingdom of God and his righteousness, and all these things will be added to you. Therefore do not be anxious about tomorrow, for tomorrow will be anxious for itself. Sufficient for the day is its own trouble."

Being anxious only causes trouble. Sometimes when we face a valley or a difficult circumstance, quoting scripture can help us trust God. An idea I have used is writing out my favorite scriptures in a place I could easily find to remind me of God and that he has the situation in his hands.

Philippians 4:4-9 (ESV) shares about trusting God and turning things over to him, "Rejoice in the Lord always; again I will say, rejoice. Let your reasonableness be known to everyone. The Lord is at hand; do not be anxious about anything, but in everything by prayer and supplication with thanksgiving let your requests be made known to God. And the peace of God, which surpasses all understanding, will guard your hearts and your minds in Christ Jesus. Finally, brothers, whatever is true, whatever is honorable, whatever is just, whatever is pure, whatever is lovely, whatever is commendable, if there is any excellence, if there is anything worthy of praise, think about these things. What you have learned and received and heard and seen in me—practice these things, and the God of peace will be with you."

How do we guard our hearts and minds? We guard them by keeping check on what we think about. If we dwell on anxious thoughts, we will be anxious. Trust the Lord with every detail of your life. He cares about everything you face, and he knows about all you face, too.

"Come now, you who say, 'Today or tomorrow we will go into such and such a town and spend a year there and trade and make a profit'—yet you do not know what tomorrow will bring. What is your life? For you are a mist that appears for a little time and then vanishes. Instead you ought to say, 'If the Lord wills, we will live and do this or that.' As it is, you boast in your arrogance. All such boasting is evil. So whoever knows the right thing to do and fails to do it, for him it is sin." (James 4:13-17 ESV)

Give what concerns you over to God. Then, we are not to just listen to God about what to do but to act on what he tells us to do.

God is a God of peace. First Corinthians 14:33 (ESV) tell us this, "For God is not a God of confusion but of peace."

Ask him for clarity if you do not understand. Gideon did this in Judges 6:11–24. Gideon was called a "mighty man of valor" even though he had not fought yet. He was confused at first, but then we find his response in verses 23–24 (ESV), "But the Lord said to him, 'Peace be to you. Do not fear; you shall not die.' Then Gideon built an altar there to the Lord and called it, The Lord Is Peace. To this day it still stands at Ophrah, which belongs to the Abiezrites." Gideon heard the Lord and found peace in him.

God gives us peace. We find this in 2 Thessalonians 3:16 (ESV) which tells us, "Now may the Lord of peace himself give you peace at all times in every way. The Lord be with you all."

God cannot look upon sin, and something had to happen to allow us to be redeemed from our sins. Jesus paved the way for us to have peace with God by dying on the cross for our sins. Colossians 1:19–20 (NIV) explains this further, "For in [Jesus] all the fullness of God was pleased to dwell, and through him to reconcile to himself all things, whether on earth or in heaven, making peace by the blood of his cross."

We are all different and unique and each of us has our own part God has called us to. "Let the peace of Christ rule in your hearts, since as members of one body you were called to peace. And be thankful" (Colossians 3:15, NIV).

How can we remember to go to God when the situation seems over-whelming? We are not alone; we were given the Holy Spirit to helps us. "But the Helper, the Holy Spirit, whom the Father will send in my name, he will teach you all things and bring to your remembrance all that I have said to you. Peace I leave with you; my peace I give to you. Not as the world gives do I give to you. Let not your hearts be troubled, neither let them be afraid" (John 14:26–27, ESV).

Go out in peace—God's peace that will keep you steadfast in all situations as you trust in him. As Jesus said, "Peace be with you."

"Eight days later, his disciples were inside again, and Thomas was with them. Although the doors were locked, Jesus came and stood among them and said, 'Peace be with you'" (John 20:26, ESV). "On the evening of that day, the first day of the week, the doors being locked where the disciples were for fear of the Jews, Jesus came and stood among them and said to them, 'Peace be with you'" (John 20:19, ESV).

So, how do you learn to trust God? It would be hard to trust someone you do not know, so you first need to get in the Bible and talk with God through prayer. Pursue peace by picking a time to meet with God. "But when you pray, go into your room and shut the door and pray to your Father who is in secret. And your Father who sees in secret will reward you" (Matthew 6:6, ESV).

Choose a place indoors or outside where you will not be distracted, and by devotions, prayer, and reading the Bible, you will get to know him more. "Whoever desires to love life and see good days, let him keep his tongue from evil and his lips from speaking deceit; let him turn away from evil and do good; let him seek peace and pursue it. For the eyes of the Lord are on the righteous, and his ears are open to their prayer. But the face of the Lord is against those who do evil" (1 Peter 3:10–12, ESV).

We are to be a peacemaker as described in Matthew 5:9 (ESV), "Blessed are the peacemakers, for they shall be called sons of God."

We can be a peacemaker by spreading peace with others, as mentioned in James 3:17–18 (ESV), "But the wisdom from above is first pure, then peaceable, gentle, open to reason, full of mercy and good fruits, impartial and sincere. And a harvest of righteousness is sown in peace by those who make peace."

Hebrews 12:12-14(ESV) adds, "Therefore lift your drooping hands and strengthen your weak knees, and make straight paths for your feet, so that what is lame may not be put out of joint but rather be healed. Strive for peace with everyone, and for the holiness without which no one will see the Lord."

A great way to be a peacemaker is to pray for others. This is important, especially if you are often with someone who is difficult to get along with. It is a lot harder to disagree with someone after you are asking the Lord to draw the person to himself or bless the person.

We all need prayer—family, friends, co-workers, and even strangers. Why? Because we want everyone to be saved and have a relationship with God just like he desires to have a relationship with each of them. "First of all, then, I urge that supplications, prayers, intercessions, and thanksgivings be made for all people, for kings and all who are in high positions, that we may lead a peaceful and quiet life, godly and dignified in every way. This is good, and it is pleasing in the sight of God our Savior, who desires all people to be saved and to come to the knowledge of the truth" (1 Timothy 2:1–4, ESV).

Who will you share your faith with?

Review Questions:
- What was Jephthah's tragic downfall?
- Why should we not be afraid?

Scripture memory verse:
Jeremiah 29:11 (ESV)

"'For I know the plans I have for you,' declares the Lord, 'plans to prosper you and not to harm you, plans to give you hope and a future.'"

Challenge:
Make a list of your "faith" moments. List times that God showed up in your life when you had faith in him.

HOPE

CHAPTER 7

Hope: Where We Start

Alone in a dark room, I buried my face in a pillow to muffle my cries. I wished that someone, anyone, would come near to ease my emotional pain and loneliness I felt during my high school years.

I sensed the Holy Spirit attempting to whisper kind words and His presence drawing near to me.

"No!" I proclaimed, "I don't want You, I want [this person] to be here." Even though that person was miles away, that was the person I imagined to be there to comfort me instead of God. I had said I wanted anyone to come, but I did not really mean it. I had dreamed for something that would never happen and simultaneously, pushed away the One who could fulfill my hope. And so, I felt hopeless.

Hopeless is a little different than helpless. On March 31, 2023, a tornado crossed through the campground I live at. It barreled down on us just before midnight. I took shelter from the storm in the bathtub with the camp dog nearby, and my friends were sheltered in other locations. One of my friends who was miles away, called me on the phone just before the tornado hit. As I was talking with her, the power went out, and the dog jumped in the bathtub onto my lap.

Suddenly, I heard the tornado. The muffled roar of it barreled down, and its telltale train sound was above my head. *It's here, it's here! I hear it.*

I told my friend, and she started praying aloud with me. I was completely helpless. I could not tell the tornado to turn to the left or to the right. I could not keep my friends safe, and I could not even keep the dog safe, little less myself. In that moment, I turned to the only One who could help: the Lord.

God is a loving Father. He desires to give us good things. He watches over us. Matthew 7:7–11 (ESV) reminds us of this, "Ask, and it will be given to you; seek, and you will find; knock and it will be open to you. For everyone who asks receives, and the one who seeks finds, and to the one who knocks, it will be opened. Or which one of you, if his son asks him for bread, will give him a stone? Or if he asks for a fish, will give him a serpent? If you then, who are evil, know how to give good gifts to your children, how much more will your Father who is in Heaven give good things to those who ask Him!"

God can be trusted!

Not only can God be trusted, but he is right there in the middle of the trial, holding us close. He is the shoulder to lean on when we are broken and falling apart. Colossians 1:17 (ESV) says, "And He is before all things, and in Him all things hold together."

He holds us together when we are crumbling apart. We do not have to feel hopeless!

God molds us and makes us into who we are meant to be. Countless people have walked away from God because he had not done what they thought he should. At any moment, God could step into our situation and pull us out of it; however, a believer may be kept in the difficult situation for an extended time. Why? Hope is built through the trials. Romans 5:3–4 (ESV) describes this further, "We rejoice in our sufferings, knowing that suffering produces endurance, and endurance produces character and character produces hope."

How can suffering produce hope in the long run? Turn with me to the end of the famous Hebrews 11 Hall of Faith chapter. "Some were tortured, refusing to accept release, so that they might rise again to a better

life. Others suffered mocking and flogging, and even chains and imprisonment. They were stoned, they were sawn in two, they were killed with
the sword. They went about in skins of sheep and goats, destitute, af-
flicted, mistreated- of whom the world was not worthy- wandering about
in deserts and mountains, and in dens and caves of the earth. And all
these, though commended through their faith, did not receive what was
promised, since God had provided something better for us, that apart
from us they should not be made perfect" (Hebrews 11:35, ESV).

The last verse says the promises they received on earth were a fore-
taste of the promises to come, which include the everlasting life we are
all eligible to receive by faith. These believers waited out the hard times;
some even refused to be released from their torture because they knew
that their reward in Heaven would make the pain all worth it. They
may have even desired to go through the struggles to show the love of
Christ to others.

Throughout my life, I have made a few trips to the emergency room.
One of my most memorable visits was due to a half-baseball sized area of
swelling on the side of my head. I was miserable and went to the walk-in
clinic to hopefully avoid an expensive emergency room trip.

After a brief inspection, the doctors told me that I needed to go to
the emergency room right away. My mom and I went to the emergency
room, and I ended up being admitted into the hospital overnight. The
ER doctors discovered an abscess close to my ear in a preauricular pit
that was filled with infection. They had an ear, nose, and throat doctor
who could see me the next day, but I needed to stay overnight.

My mom left around midnight. Before she left, she turned on the TV
for me so that I could be entertained. She also gave me my purse so I could
have all the essentials I needed during my stay, then she left.

I pulled my Bible out of my purse and I read and read. That night
was one of the worst nights I have ever experienced. Every few hours, the
nurses would come in and check my vitals and see if I needed more medicine. I was in constant, intense pain and cried throughout the night. I had

to visit a communal restroom down the hall several times. On one of my trips back to my room, I overheard the overnight staff referring to me and why I was there, as I had already passed them multiple times. I felt so miserable and helpless. I am sure they wanted to help me just as much as I wished they could.

The book of the Bible that I read the most that night was Job. I could relate to experiencing painful suffering and feeling alone. Every time I started to feel lonely and helpless, I called out to God to intervene in my situation. I clung to Job 13:15 (ESV) that says, "Though he slay me, I will hope in him."

Even though I was in severe pain, I knew that in God was still my hope. Even though I needed to wait until the next day before I could have some relief, I knew that God was in control and that I could trust him. And I realized that even if I did not make it through the night, I knew God was still watching over me.

Early the next morning, the ear, nose, and throat doctor removed most of the infection and packed my ear with gauze. I ended up battling the infection for several months, and even three years later, I still had to have surgery on my ear again before the pain was completely gone.

But, my friend I want you to know, I know where my hope lies. It is in the Lord everlasting, who is our mighty protector. I may be helpless to change a situation, but God is not. Whether or not the outcome will be as I anticipate, God is still on the throne. He holds my situation in his hand and promises to go through it with me.

I hoped God would stop the pain I battled from the abscess. I hoped God would keep me safe in the tornado. Yet, even if God had not changed my situations, my hope is in God, and I look forward to his promised eternal life.

Our hope is not for this life alone. I hoped that I would be kept safe and pain free, but my hope was not in the circumstance, it was in Jesus. First Corinthians 15:19 (ESV) tells us this, "If in Christ we have hope in this life only, we are of all people most to be pitied."

Our hope comes from God, and it rests in eternal life. When we pass from this earth to the eternal life to come, we will be clothed with the things that are imperishable or everlasting. "When the perishable puts on the imperishable, and the moral puts on immorality, then shall come to pass the saying that is written: 'Death is swallowed up in victory.' O death, where is your victory? O death, where is your sting?'" (1 Corinthians 15:54–55, ESV)

What made the sting of death vanquished? Perhaps "who" is the better question, for it was Jesus who triumphed over death. "The sting of death is sin, and the power of sin is the law. But thanks be to God, who gives us the victory through our Lord Jesus Christ" (1 Corinthians 15:56–57, ESV)

Death no longer has a hold on God's children, because we are born again. We will receive an inheritance in Heaven and eternal life. First Peter 1:3–9 (ESV) says, "Blessed be the God and Father of our Lord Jesus Christ! According to his great mercy, he has caused us to be born again to a living hope through the resurrection of Jesus Christ from the dead, to an inheritance that is imperishable, undefiled, and unfading, kept in heaven for you, who by God's power are being guarded through faith for a salvation ready to be revealed in the last time. In this you rejoice, though now for a little while, if necessary, you have been grieved by various trials, so that the tested genuineness of your faith- more precious than gold that perishes thought it is tested by fire—may be found to result in praise and glory and honor at the revelation of Jesus Christ. Though you have not seen him, you love him. Though you do not now see him, you believe in him and rejoice with joy that is inexpressible and filled with glory, obtaining the outcome of your faith, the salvation of your souls."

Because we have faith, we can have hope. Hope is our heartbeat: it keeps us going. It anchors us to Jesus. "We have this hope as an anchor for the soul, firm and secure" (Hebrews 6:19, NIV). Hope tethers us to the Lord. Since we have hope in life after death, we can be strong in the Lord in our daily living, knowing that staying close to Jesus will be worth it in the end.

Hope makes a difference in us. It helps us to be bold and steadfast no matter what life throws our way. "Since we have such a hope, we are very bold," (2 Corinthians 3:12, ESV).

Hope kept Shadrach, Meshach, and Abednego strong in faith when they faced the fiery furnace in Daniel 3. We can find no record of these men receiving instruction from the Lord about what to do once they reached the fiery furnace, yet they stood firm in their faith in God and knowledge of God's will, even in the face of death. They did not waiver in their belief, knowing full well their lives were on the line.

My story is one of redemption and hope. I began as a Christian at a young age and then drifted far away from God into a pit of hopelessness. One day, I returned to God and chose him to be Lord over my life.

I have come from deep depression and have been brought out into marvelous life filled with hope. God still saves. God still changes lives. God still redeems. If God could change me, a broken wanderer who was running in the opposite direction from him, then he can change you too.

I love what Paul says in 1 Corinthians 15:9, "For I am the least of the apostles, unworthy to be called an apostle, because I persecuted the church of God." And Ephesians 3:8–9 (ESV), "To me, though I am the very least of all the saints, this grace was given, to preach to the Gentiles the unsearchable riches of Christ, and to bring to light for everyone what is the plan of the mystery hidden for ages in God, who created all things."

I, too, think of myself as the least of all the saints. I purposefully turned away from God and his will. Even though I was not taking others' lives, like Paul did, I nearly took my own and would have missed out on all that God had for me later. You might feel like this, too, in your own story.

God often turns to the "least of these" to do his will. Those who are "full of themselves" do not have enough space in their hearts to let the Lord in.

The "least of these" tend to be humble and recognize that by God alone, they can do what he has called them to do. Gideon was one of the "least of these," as he shared in Judges 6:15 (ESV), "And he said to him, 'Please, Lord, how can I save Israel? Behold, my clan is the weakest in Manasseh, and I am the least in my father's house.'"

In Heaven least and greatest are opposite of the way we see here on earth. Matthew 11:11 (ESV) puts it this way, "Truly, I say to you, among those born of women there has arisen no one greater than John the Baptist. Yet the one who is least in the kingdom of heaven is greater than he."

Do you know who else came from the "least of these?" Luke 2:4-12 (NIV) says, "So Joseph also went up from the town of Nazareth in Galilee to Judea, to Bethlehem the town of David, because he belonged to the house and line of David. He went there to register with Mary, who was pledged to be married to him and was expecting a child. While they were there, the time came for the baby to be born, and she gave birth to her firstborn, a son. She wrapped him in cloths and placed him in a manger, because there was no guest room available for them. And there were shepherds living out in the fields nearby, keeping watching over their flocks at night. An angel of the Lord appeared to them, and the glory of the Lord shone around them, and they were terrified, But the angel said to them, 'Do not be afraid. I bring you good news that will cause great joy for all the people. Today in the town of David a Savior has been born to you; he is the Messiah, the Lord. This will be a sign to you: You will find a baby wrapped in cloths and lying in a manger.'"

Jesus, the King of kings and Lord of lords, was born through humble circumstances. He was born after the long trek to another city called Bethlehem and placed in a livestock manger. The birth of the King of kings was told to the shepherds out in the fields with their sheep. They did not have time to get cleaned up to meet the Messiah. These men were probably dirty and smelly, but God chose them to meet his son. God is not afraid to get down and dirty in our mess.

Jesus is also the good shepherd, and the shepherds who came to worship him at his birth mirrored Jesus' own life. "I am the good shepherd.

The good shepherd lays down his life for the sheep" (John 10:11, ESV). God used the shepherds to show the correlation between how a shepherd tends to his sheep and how God lovingly tends to his children.

Remember the dog that was in the bathtub with me during the tornado? Her name is Holly. My friends called her Holly Hope when she was first adopted—when my friends rescued her several years ago, and she was matted and beaten from her previous owner. My friends paid for the surgery to fix Holly's mangled mouth and to get the mats removed so she could walk again. They helped her get to the point where on the outside she looked like a regular dog.

However, a male had abused her, and because of this, on the inside, she was terrified of men. My friends were not able to keep her with them since she was terrified of the husband because he was a man. Holly cowered in the corner and shook whenever he was around.

So, Holly came to live with us at our house at the campground. She was still afraid of men and would run whenever the man at her new house moved. Anytime he stood up, Holly ran behind the couch. If a slight sound was made, Holly ran behind the couch. In Holly's new environment, she was able to hide in a young woman's room at one end of the house. Holly Hope did not have to be around the man in the house if she did not want to, and she had found herself a safe place. We were all the more determined to shower Holly with affection to let her know that she was indeed loved by us all.

I remember the first time Holly played with me. I was in the backyard with her, and she jumped in a kiddie pool and then took off running around the yard. I acted like I was going to catch her and then she rushed past me. She was beginning to grow. After her first year, she had made some small improvements. She was okay with men if they sat very still and did not make a sound. My friends who rescued Holly Hope wanted to use her story to teach a group of young teenagers about hope. My friends had everyone sit very still and told them not make any sudden movements.

At the time, Holly did not like to leave her corner of the campground, and it was a major struggle for me to coax her over the side door of the building, where the teenagers were waiting. I was sitting outside the door with Holly, praying that God would calm her nerves and that she would be willing to go inside. If Holly did not decide to enter the room on her own, I was to take her back home. My friends had decided that they would let her choose.

As I sat there praying and petting Holly Hope, I had peace that God was going to work it all out.

My friends cued me, and as I opened the door, Holly decided to walk inside. I held my breath as she walked to the seated teenagers and allowed one or two to pet her. One of the people she walked right up to was my friend, who was a guy. I wanted to shout for joy.

After a few minutes Holly Hope returned to me, and I quietly led her back home. Once we were outside, I cheered and told her how proud I was of her. I thanked the Lord for allowing her to be used to share about hope.

You see, Holly Hope did not have to change. She could have chosen to stay the same as when she arrived at camp. Yet, with being surrounded by love and in a new environment, Holly grew in leaps and bounds. Today, she likes to lie in the middle of the living room so that everyone must step around her. Yes, even the guys. Holly also howls when she is excited or ready to eat. She plays with tennis balls and stuffed toys, and her favorite thing to do is go on a car ride with the man from her newer house.

Holly is a perfect example of how a new, loving environment can change someone. She is a wonderful illustration of how God's love and promise of a new life can create hope in someone.

Perhaps we, too, were afraid of certain people. Perhaps we, too, were afraid to laugh and have fun. Perhaps we, too, were from an abusive environment. Perhaps we, too, had given up all hope that we would get a chance at a new life. Perhaps we, too, were like Holly; maybe we were discouraged and gave up, until we chose God and he pulled us up out of the pit to set us on the firm foundation of Jesus Christ. He then showered us with his life-changing love and gave us someone to put our hope in. That is where Jesus comes in. He is our hope.

When I was in the bathtub during the tornado, clutching my Bible for dear life, I knew that if I made it out alive, my Bible would be the one possession I would need to get through life. I have heard stories of believers in other nations who memorize as much of the Bible as they can every time they have one, because Bibles are quickly taken away or destroyed.

I, too, want to hold on tightly to my Bible as they do in some of these countries. I want to rely on it every day to get me though. I want to memorize portions of scripture so that when I am in the battle, I can quote it and bring it to mind.

That day the tornado had caused our house to rattle, I had held my pillow over my head praying, "Lord, keep us all safe."

As quickly as the tornado had begun, it had passed by. I received another alert on my phone that a second tornado was heading in our direction, so I stayed sheltered for nearly an hour. When I finally emerged, the damage was unusual. Our home was nearly untouched with only a shutter ripped off the wall and a plastic outdoor dining set missing. My friends began gathering from shelters and we went to access the damages.

The gym was the first damaged building we saw. The tornado had touched down on the roof of the gym, and a fifth of the roof was laid over on the top of the building like it was a turned page on a book. Inside the gym, the basketball goal was detached from the wall and hung sideways. Cement bricks from the wall were either missing or turned sideways.

Throughout the rest of the campground, trees had fallen several different directions, debris was scattered throughout the trees, the lightbulbs in a couple of strands of outdoor lights had exploded, and a shed was moved a foot over.

It seemed like everywhere we looked, we saw damage. The next day, we discovered that the dormitory building behind our house had the roof torn off the west end. By following the damages of the storm, it appears that the tornado had jumped over our house and the dorm be-side us and touched down on the gym at the other end of the camp.

Not one of the camp volunteers was injured. In fact, the buildings we were sheltering in were all kept safe. God is so good. He fulfilled our hope and kept us safe. But, even if we had not made it through the night, we knew where we were going.

The Lord can turn our life around in an instant. In my life, changes began happening rapidly within the first few months after I had accepted the Lord. Even still, some changes happened quickly and some have taken a lot more time. One of the quickest changes was when I wanted to be baptized. At the end of the summer of 2012, I was baptized by my new friends at the camp.

In the event of baptism, we see a physical display on the outside, showing what has occurred inside of someone. The person being bap-tized is saying, "I believe and I am not afraid of the consequences of following Christ. I am not keeping this life change to myself, and you are my witnesses."

In some countries overseas believers know that being baptized could be a death sentence. To say that they are Christians goes against the majority religion, and by being baptized, the others will know ex-actly whom to target. Even here in America, many are criticized or even ostracized when they turn to the Lord. It is a choice we need to make even when it is difficult to do so.

Jesus knew he would meet opposition when he came to save the earth. Even though he knew that, he still chose to die on the cross for our sins.

Will we choose Jesus even when doing so is hard? Will we still have hope in Him, even when our lives are crumbling all around us? Will we cling to the cross and its reminder that Jesus suffered first? Jesus does not ask us to do what he did not do first.

First Peter 3:14-22 (ESV) points to this, "But even if you should suffer for righteousness' sake, you will be blessed. Have no fear of them, nor be troubled, but in your hearts honor Christ the Lord as holy, always being prepared to make defense to anyone who asks you for a reason for the hope that is in you; yet do it with gentleness and respect, having good conscience, so that, when you are slandered, those who revile your good behavior in Christ may be put to shame. For it is better to suffer for doing good, if that should be God's will, than for doing evil. For Christ also suffered once for sins, the righteous for the unrighteous, that he might bring us to God, being put to death in the flesh but made alive in the spirit, in which he went and proclaimed to the spirits in prison, because they formerly did not obey, when God's patience waited in the days of Noah, while the ark was being prepared, in which a few, that is, eight persons, were brought safely through water. Baptism, which corresponds to this, now saves you, not as a removal of dirt from the body but as an appeal to God for good conscience, through the resurrection of Jesus Christ, who has gone into heaven and is at the right hand of God, with angels, authorities, and powers having been subjected to him."

I like the way my *NIV Study Bible* describes this reference to baptism. "Baptism saves only in the sense that it represents what Christ has achieved. The waters of the Noahic flood symbolize baptism, and baptism is the sign and seal of salvation 'by the resurrection of Jesus Christ' (See Romans 6:4). Baptism is not merely a religious ritual that washes the body; it is one's pledge to God to live righteously from that time on, which results in a clear conscience before him. Peter reminds his readers of the pledge of their baptism at a time when they are facing suffering because of Christ and are tempted to turn away from the Lord."[xvi]

I remember the day I was baptized during that summer many years ago. It seemed like every time I read the Bible leading to that day, it mentioned baptism, and I could hardly wait to be baptized. It was a beautiful, warm, summer day, and my dear friends filled the horse trough with water that morning.

When it was time for the baptism, they were gathered around me, and we sang "Amazing Grace." One of the camp directors baptized me in the still brisk, cold water. I remember that the water was refreshing, and I felt like I had taken a deep breath while standing outside in winter.

After I came up out of the water, the director asked me if I had a word to say. I responded, "I am not sure what God is going to do with me, but I am looking forward to being used by him."

God has a plan for our lives. He has a plan for each one of us if we will choose to be used by him. How exciting to think of the day we reach Heaven and hear the precious words, "Well done good and faithful servant" (Matthew 25:21, ESV). It would certainly be better than hearing, "I never knew you; depart from me, you workers of lawlessness." (Matthew 7:23, ESV).

I am aiming for the "well done," and I hope you are too. Life with God is a journey, and we get to our destination if we walk with him.

Review Questions:

- What is the difference between hopeless and helpless?
- Where does our hope come from?

Scripture memory verse:

Hebrews 6:19 (ESV)

"We have this hope as an anchor for the soul, firm and secure."

Challenge:

How can you focus on Jesus in the hard and seemingly hopeless situations? Write out some ideas you can put into practice to shift your focus back on him.

CHAPTER 8

Hope: As We Grow

The year 2020 brought a lot of change for me. Not only was the entire world facing an epidemic, but also, I had been in a car wreck that totaled my car, and I was looking for a new car in the midst of the pandemic. I was also looking for a new church to attend. I hoped to find one that had some younger people in attendance because most of my closest friends were in their fifties and sixties, and I needed to also be with others my own age.

My grandparents had been attending a church for a while and then my friends, the camp directors, began attending the same church. My friends invited me to join them, but I hesitated because I was looking for a church with younger individuals, and most young people did not attend churches that my grandparents or older friends attended. Nonetheless, I decided to check it out after my friends said that several of our camp friends also attended there.

When I arrived at the church, the congregation was not in their normal sanctuary because their building needed repair. Instead, we met in a beautiful, older-style church with stained glass windows and wooden pews lining the sanctuary.

During one of my first visits to this church, I met twin girls who were only a few years younger than me. This church was similar to the church

I had attended as a young child, with hymns and an older congregation, and I quickly felt at peace about attending there. I looked forward to the weekly chats with my new friends after church services.

One day, when I was leaving after service, my pastor introduced me to the twins' older brother. We spoke for a minute or two and went our separate ways. In the middle of 2023, the young man and I started talking, found many similarities, and soon began dating.

By this point in my life, I had given up on falling in love and dating again. After a few relationships, I told myself that since I have been in ministry, I was just going to be single and be devoted to God alone for the rest of my life. That was until, "I found him whom my soul loves" (Song of Solomon 3:4, ESV).

While we do not know what God has in store for us, we know we will trust in his plan. We are still taking each step waiting on God's will and we are now engaged. I had lost hope that I would ever date again, but God was not done yet, and I found I could fall in love again. We are taking each day one at a time, but how wonderful it is to be able to dream again and have hope for the future!

Had I mentioned the name of my church yet? It is Hope—Hope Community Church. How aptly named for many reasons, but for me, it was especially coincidental for the hope that God returned to my heart.

If you are facing a similar situation and wondering if God has someone out there for you, please know, my friend, that there is hope for you, too. There may not be someone out there that God has in mind for you to date, but we can put our hope in God, and that he will work everything out even when we do not understand.

I learned a while ago from some of my dear friends that they had each prayed for God to lead them to someone they would spend the rest of their lives with. They knew so many people who entered bad relationships or divorced early into their marriages, so they prayed that if they married, they would stay married. God has good plans for us, whether or not they include marriage, and as we walk closely with him, we get to live in them.

Our hope comes from the Lord, just like our help does. When I was young, I was afraid of many things. I still remember the day I saw my own shadow and was terrified! I was very young, but I still remember that it kept following me, and I could not get away.

I also used to have nightmares or a bad dream every night, and I would pray "Lord, please help me not to have nightmares or bad dreams."

Many years later when I was in college, I found Psalm 121, wrote it out, and stuck it under my pillow. Eventually, I stopped having as many nightmares and bad dreams, after I rededicated my life to Christ.

Psalm 121 (ESV) says, "I lift up my eyes to the hills. From where does my help come? My help comes from the Lord, who made heaven and earth. He will not let your foot be moved; he who keeps you will not slumber. Behold, he who keeps Israel will neither slumber nor sleep. The Lord is your keeper; the Lord is your shade on your right hand. The sun shall not strike you by day, nor the moon by night. The Lord will keep you from all evil; he will keep your life. The Lord will keep your going out and your coming in from this time forth and forevermore."

God was going to take care of me; I just had to trust him.

Trust and faith go hand in hand, and hope is the byproduct.

I remember a soccer game I played in during high school. It was our opposing teams' senior night, which basically meant they were celebrating the high school seniors before they left for college. It was a big deal for the home team to win the senior night's game.

When I was playing soccer, my position often became a "man-to-man" play. I would be assigned to the best player on the other team, and my job was to shut that person down. I was to keep the ball away from the person or to take it away as quickly as possible. The girl on the other team I was "man marking," was one of the seniors, but not only that, she had become my friend over the years.

I had played against her many times before, and out of all of the other players that I was assigned to, she was the only one that became my friend. That day I had mentioned to her that I remembered her from the years before, and when the ball was at the other end of the field, we talked about where she was going to college.

My team won that day, and for one of the first times, I felt bad for the other team. We parted ways, and she went on to celebrate her senior night with her team. She is married now with a good job, and I still see her on social media every once in a while. I had hoped that her team would win, but God had another plan, and in doing so, he taught me a lesson that day. I had always hoped that we would win, but this time I hoped that they would instead. My perspective had shifted to hoping that God would show up in their situation instead.

We can get so caught up in hoping for things to go well in our lives, that we can forget that someone else might need the "win" this time. We need to use wisdom and discernment in these times and see where God is leading us to pray and hope.

When I first started playing soccer, I was the only girl in my age group. I played soccer on an all-boys team for a few years and then played with an older girls' team. Our team lost most of our games, if not all of them.

When my family moved to another state, I began playing soccer on a team with other girls my age. I remember that when we lost one of our first games, it bothered my teammates. I was confused because my previous team often lost our games, and I had become accustomed to losing. I still remember the first game my new team won. I was dumbfounded. *We won? We actually won a game!*

As the years went by, we lost some games and won others. I had gotten to the point where I greatly enjoyed winning soccer games over losing. One day while I was playing on my high school soccer team, we were losing, and it was a game I had really hoped we would win. I prayed, *Lord, please help us win! Please. Please.*

Then, the Holy Spirit whispered to me, *What if they are praying to win too? Who should I let win?*

I paused and thought, *Oh, well I didn't think of it like that.*

I had hoped that God would step in and help us win, but I ended up with empathy for the other team instead. The Lord was opening my heart to begin to think of others and their needs.

Yes, God cares about us and the things that matter to us, and this game mattered to me, but he also sees his children and what they truly need. I did not need our team to win that game, I wanted it. My view of God at that time was like a genie. *God I need this, can you help?*

But God was calling out my name the whole time, saying, I want *you* instead. He knew my heart was far from him. I remember many times when I could not find something in my room. I would pray, *God can you help me find this? If so, I will do better at following you. I'll live for you.*

Every time God helped me find something, I thanked him, but I had not rededicated my life to him yet, and I continually fell back into my old ways. My hope was not really in God; it was still in the world and worldly things.

In whom or what do we put our hope? People? Money? Our own strength? God? If we choose to put our hope in God, he will come through for us every time, even if he does not do so in the way we expect.

I expected God to step in and change the way that the soccer game was playing out. But instead, God stepped in and helped me see the other person as someone he loves, too. He helped me see a friend in an opponent on her senior night, and he still teaches me that even an enemy still needs Jesus. We all do. Having our hope in God transforms us into being more like him.

When we put our faith and hope in God, we are not shaken up, as we were beforehand. We receive supernatural peace that can quiet any storm, even the one inside us. "God is our refuge and strength, a very present help in trouble. Therefore we will not fear though the earth gives way, though the mountains be moved into the heart of the sea, though its waters roar and foam, though the mountains trembles at its swelling. Selah" (Psalm 46:1–3, ESV). We have the peace of God quieting our hearts.

Making a list of times when God came through for you and me can be very uplifting and encouraging. It can help us remember that God had not left us then, and he will not leave us now. He is there in the trouble and will be there in the next time of trouble, too. And miracles are still very possible.

Almost ten years ago, I fell in love with a song that I would eventually call my testimony. It is the song "Redeemed" by Big Daddy Weave. The song talks about being redeemed from the chains of our past and God gives us a new name and he will give us hope that will help us until the end.[xvii]

Years ago, I went to a Big Daddy Weave concert. At the end of the night, some of the band and crew lined the front of the stage, and they invited people down for prayer. I wanted to go up and seek prayer for a desire I had to be a missionary to China. I had recently returned from going on a mission trip there and wanted to return soon.

I went up for prayer to one of the crew, and he asked me my name. I said "Brooke" very quickly. At the time, I thought I had other things I was ready to get to and tell him about.

He said, "What?"

"Brooke," I responded just as quickly as before.

"Do you like your name?" He asked me.

"No. I mean I'm glad my parents gave me a name, but . . . "

"What does you name mean?" He asked.

"A stream, running water, but it also means to bear and to suffer."

"I am going to pray that God tells you the name he has for you." And he prayed so.

It was a totally unexpected turn of events.

The next day, I was driving the two hours to camp from Illinois, which I did frequently and had become a bi-weekly time of prayer and talking with the Lord for me. Can you guess what I was avoiding the entire time?

I finally gave in and prayed, "Lord if you have a name for me, can you please tell me what it is?"

No sooner than the words came, I had a vision of an angel, so big that I could only see its chest and arms! In its hands, a small scroll was slowly opened, and on it I saw the letters F A Y I N. It looked like something was above the "a" and something above the "i." I thought that the "a" was the letter " ä " and the "i" was a standard "i."

When I got to camp, I looked up Fäyin and found . . . *nothing!* So, I just typed in those five letters, F A Y I N and suddenly a ton of websites written in CHINESE popped up! So I took the word I saw there, fāyīn, and looked that up. And guess what fāyīn meant? Pronunciation. Anticlimactic, right?

So, I split up the two tones, Fā and Yīn and looked at what each of those meant. Fā means "to send out" and yīn means "voice." On that day, God gave me not only a name like he had given Peter and Paul, but a calling on my life—to be a voice sent out into the world to share about him.

My calling is like yours, too, if you are a believer. You may know it as the Great Commission. "Go therefore and make disciples of all nations, baptizing them in the name of the Father and of the Son and of the Holy Spirit, teaching them to observe all that I have commanded you. And behold, I am with you always, to the end of the age" (Matthew 28:19–20, ESV).

In January of 2021, Fayin Teaching Ministries began as a means to reach people for the glory of God through speaking and writing. I still go by Brooke because I am thankful my parents gave me my name, but I am also thankful that God also showed me his name for me and so the ministry's name was born. God has blessed me more than I deserve.

This past year, I was able to give Big Daddy Weave's lead singer, Mike, my story written out on a piece of paper and also share about it with him. What a God moment! All these years later, I was able to share with the host of that prayer time what had happened through it! It really came full circle, and I'm so thankful that God opened up this opportunity.

Have you been redeemed by God? Has he changed your life in such a way that it is nearly unrecognizable from the way it looked before he came into your life?

Hope in the Lord will carry us, not watch us nor leave us.

The amazing part was when I received my name from the Lord, I had already been in college for a couple years, trying to find the right career path. And after rededicating my life to the Lord a couple of years prior, my priorities had quickly shifted, and I still was on the lookout for the job God was calling me to. So, this new possible career path I thought I was going to mention to the man who prayed with me at the concert? Over time, God showed me that it was not going to be a good job for me, and I once again switched careers. He knows me better than I know myself. So, when I thought God was calling me to the overseas mission field, instead he was calling me to another mission field altogether . . . reaching my neighbor.

When I was talking with lead singer, Mike, this past year, he told me of an overseas trip he will be going on. We talked about the brave men and women overseas who risk their lives to share the gospel even if it will cost them their own lives.

Going overseas is always nerve-wracking, but even more so when it's a country where Christians are not welcomed by most of the population. Anytime we travel someplace when our life is going to be on the line or even as a believer just trying to make it through each day here in our own country, we should ask ourselves the same question found in the "Love: As We Grow" chapter, the same question the missionary asked me, "Are you willing to die for Jesus?" Because, *that's all that matters.*

Years ago, a believer in China had the largest underground house church in the country. His name was Pastor Lamb, and the house church was so large that the authorities could not destroy it. Pastor Lamb was arrested, and every day the guards would come to him and say, "Your friends have already renounced Christ, you should too." And they would beat him after he refused to deny Christ.

One day, a fellow believer in the jail started singing "The Old Rugged Cross." The guards beat the man. Soon another believer started singing, followed by another, and Pastor Lamb joined in. He knew he was not alone, and that the guards had lied, the men had not renounced Christ after all! The guards came and beat each of the men, but the men did not retaliate for they had been encouraged and knew their suffering was for Christ.

Pastor Lamb had his hope renewed because God showed him that he was not alone. Sometimes we can feel like the only believer. The only one at work, the only one in your family, the only one on the team, but God always has a remnant of his people, and sometimes he shows us when we need extra encouragement. Maybe it is not a co-worker, but a customer who comes in that shares the love of Christ with you. Maybe you did not know anyone in your family or on your team believed, but then God revealed it in a conversation that someone did, in fact, believe. Even if not there, perhaps in your neighborhood, perhaps in your school, or in your grocery trip, you will realize that someone there believes.

Romans 11:1–5 (ESV) says, "I ask, then, has God rejected his people? By no means! For I myself am an Israelite, a descendant of Abraham, a member of the tribe of Benjamin. God has not rejected his people whom he foreknew. Do you not know what the Scripture says of Elijah, how he appeals to God against Israel? 'Lord, they have killed your prophets, they have demolished your altars, and I alone am left, and they seek my life.' But what is God's reply to him? 'I have kept for myself seven thousand men who have not bowed the knee to Baal.' So too at the present time there is a remnant, chosen by grace."

God leaves a remnant. Even when it looks bleak and like you are all alone, you are not. Just as Pastor Lamb discovered, even though the guards said no one was left, there were enough left for a short, sponta-neous worship service.

This moment encouraged the believers and helped their hope grow in some place as seemingly hopeless as a prison. Do you know where

Philippians, the most joyful book of the Bible, was written? In a prison. Paul encouraged the believers to rejoice no matter their circumstances. Philippians 4:4–7 (ESV) tells us, "Rejoice in the Lord always; again I will say, rejoice. Let your reasonableness be known to everyone. The Lord is at hand; do not be anxious about anything, but in everything by prayer and supplication with thanksgiving let your requests be made known to God. And the peace of God, which surpasses all understanding, will guard your hearts and your minds in Christ Jesus."

But Paul was in prison when he wrote this. In Philippians 1:7 (ESV), he explained, "It is right for me to feel this way about you all, because I hold you in my heart, for you are all partakers with me of grace, both in my imprisonment and in the defense and confirmation of the gospel."

I do not know about you, but I think "rejoice" and "prison" do not seem like they should go together. Paul was a prisoner because of his witness for Christ. And he had hope that the Lord was going to be with him because he had remained faithful to the Lord, whether that meant staying on this earth or moving to Heaven. He knew the Lord and his heart, and Paul was walking the right path.

One of my favorite passages of the Bible is in Psalms. Psalm 119:40–56 (ESV) says, "Remember your word to your servant, in which you have made me hope. This is my comfort in my affliction, that your promise gives me life. The insolent utterly deride me, but I do not turn away from your law. When I think of your rules from of old, I take comfort, O Lord. Hot indignation seizes me because of the wicked, who forsake your law. Your statutes have been my songs in the house of my sojourning. I remember your name in the night, O Lord, and keep your law. This blessing has fallen to me, that I have kept your precepts."

The Bible contains the Word and laws the Lord uses to give us hope and comfort. In it we see how others have fought the good fight and made it through. We see when God stepped in to save many of them. As we follow Jesus and the instructions found in the Bible, we walk the right path, even when it means others will tease or persecute us for it.

We will experience moments that help our hope grow. Those moments may come when God intervenes in our situation. As we grow, our faith and hope grow too. We can hope again for the next time that God will come through. But even if not, we know he is still good and will walk through any difficulties with us. That is where we have faith.

We will all face hard times; ones that make us not want to get up in the morning or face life. We all struggle with having hope, but God gives us hope. Turn to him, and trust him through it.

Just before Jesus was crucified, he said, "I have said these things to you, that in me you may have peace. In the world you will have tribulation. But take heart; I have overcome the world" (John 16:33, ESV). Jesus has already won the battle between good and evil. He has already overcome the world! And, by daily trusting and walking with him, we, too, can walk full of hope and see the victory he brings in our own lives. We grow in hope day by day.

Review Questions

- Who or what do you put your hope in?
- Where is God sending you to be a voice that shares about him in this world?

Scripture memory verse:

Psalm 46:1–3 (ESV)

"God is our refuge and strength, a very present help in trouble. Therefore we will not fear though the earth gives way, though the mountains be moved into the heart of the sea, though its waters roar and foam, though the mountains trembles at its swelling. Selah."

Challenge:

Pray and ask God to encourage you in your hard situation; whether it is him revealing another believer to you or giving you the peace and the ability to rejoice even if nothing changed.

CHAPTER 9

Hope: Where We Are Heading

In November of 2023, I was diagnosed with hyperthyroidism. I had never heard of hyperthyroidism before, but suddenly all of the health issues I had been experiencing were making sense. My hands had been shaking like I had tremors. I had gained weight because of an increased appetite. I was fatigued and not sleeping well, as well as having high blood pressure. I had also noticed an increased sensitivity to heat, among other hyperthyroidism systems.

There are a few different options for curing hyperthyroidism: medication, radiation, and a surgery to remove all or part of the thyroid glands. One possible complications of the surgery is damage to the vocal cords. I already had trouble speaking due to the thyroid nodule pressing on my vocal cords, and I could not imagine permanent damage to the vocal cords.

In the last chapter, I shared my story of how God gave me a new name, Fayin. Fā means "to send out" and yīn means "voice." Remember how I shared that on that day, God gave me not only a name like he had given Peter and Paul, but a calling on my life, to be a voice sent out into the world to share about him?

Suddenly I was afraid, *God, you gave me this voice to share about you! What am I supposed to do if I lose it? What if I have to learn sign language?*

What if my voice changes and never returns to normal? What if I can never tell my boyfriend that I love him again? What if? What if? What if?

The *what ifs* can be crippling if we let them be. We need to turn over our *what ifs* to God, so that they become *even ifs* instead. *Even if I lose my voice, I will still praise you. Even if I have to communicate through sign language, I will share about you. Even if my voice changes and never returns to normal, I will still use it to praise your name. Even if I can never tell my boyfriend that I love him again, I can write. I can write it a thousand times and write praises to you, Lord, ten thousand more.*

"Even if" is really "what if" with a little faith boost in between.

How can we possibly have faith that God will make it all alright? He has before. He has millions of times before. But here is where another *even if* comes in, *even if not,* I will still praise him. Even if not, I will still trust him. Even if not, he is still good! Why? Because, God can step in and change the situation, but even if he does not, he has promised to walk through it with us. And one day, we get the prize of our faith; being with the Lord in Heaven! Whether in Heaven or on Earth, God will be with those who are faithful to him. "For 'everyone who calls on the name of the Lord will be saved,'" (Romans 10:13, ESV). He saves. Jesus saves.

Jesus is the ultimate example of hope and trusting God, even when our situation looks bleak. The men at the foot of the cross mocked Jesus as he hung there dying. "And the people stood by, watching, but the rulers scoffed at him, saying, 'He saved others; let him save himself if he is the Christ of God, his Chosen One!' The soldiers also mocked him, coming up and offering him sour wine and saying, 'If you are the King of the Jews, save yourself!'" (Luke 23:35–37, ESV).

Jesus went to the cross and bore the weight of our sin, and the Father cannot look upon sin. So, the Father could not be with or look at Jesus as he hung upon the cross. God is pure and good. He cannot be with sin. No good Father would be able to turn his back on the suffering his Son went through, except for the fact that Jesus took on himself the sin of the world that the Heavenly Father could not look upon.

Jesus was innocent, yet he stood in the gap, a great chasm that was between us and the Father, and made a path so that we could have a way to be forgiven. The Father was then able to look at us, because Jesus took our place. So, when God looks at us, his children that are forgiven, he sees the righteousness of his Son, the one who took the darkness of our sins.

God knew that this was the only way to restore us to him. And Jesus said in John 10:17–18 (ESV), "For this reason the Father loves me, because I lay down my life that I may take it up again. No one takes it from me, but I lay it down of my own accord. I have the authority to lay it down, and I have the authority to take it up again. This charge I have received from my Father."

Jesus had asked his Father to take away the cup from him while he was in the Garden of Gethsemane, but Jesus was still willing to do God's will. "And going a little farther he fell on his face and prayed, saying, 'My Father if it be possible, let this cup pass from me; nevertheless, not as I will, but as you will'" (Matthew 26:39, ESV).

Jesus chose to lay his life into the Father's hands and trust him and his plans, even if that meant Jesus would endure pain and suffering. Why? Because, Jesus knew the Father and his heart and knew that God had a perfect plan.

God's perfect plan looked like death for Jesus, but salvation for the world, specifically those who chose to believe. This opened the door so the Jews and anyone else in the whole world who wanted God as their Lord and Savior, would simply need to ask Jesus to come into their life and believe in him.

Jesus' darkest moment brought the world the brightest light. Hope. We can each now experience hope because we now can have salvation and eternal life. We only had to believe.

The last thing I want to do is go through surgery, but the first thing I am going to do is to trust God. I have so far been able to keep my thyroid stable through medication. Trusting God may have taken some tears and inner wrestling, but I know God has his hand on this, and even if not, he is still good.

For countless years, the enemy has tried to silence God's people. Many of God's people died for the choices they made; others are silenced through misguided laws and unfair regulations, and even prison sentences are given for those who persisted in spreading the word about God.

Now more than ever, being quiet looks like the "good way out." However, if we see someone suffering for what is right, we should stand beside them. A good country has good rules and regulations to guide the people well. We should always be praying that our leaders listen to God and follow him and his law as they govern this nation, no matter who is in the office.

In China, the government church does not speak about the second coming of Christ, along with other missing information, or allow children to know the Bible. When I visited the country, we went to foreign churches instead of Chinese churches. We were in the country of China, and yet, the Chinese people could not even attend the churches we visited, due to the strict rules of the government forbidding them to know the true gospel.

The government church services are filled without hope. How can their children have hope when they do not know the One that gives us hope? How can the people have hope when they do not know more is coming one day or that Jesus will return? Or that judgment will come to those who do not believe and an eternal reward to those that do? There is so much more than this life.

Remember Job? "Though he slay me, I will hope in him" (Job 13:15, ESV). Why would we still trust in God when he allows bad things to happen? It is because our trust depends on our knowing the character of God. We are not immune to suffering, but God promises to give it a purpose.

I would have never thought that finding out I have an issue with my thyroid would lead to remembering that I need to throw my worries and cares onto Jesus, and perhaps these words of encouragement can help one of you too.

BUILDING ON A CHRIST-CENTERED FOUNDATION | 141

We have each been given a voice. What are you going to do with yours? Are you going to share about Jesus and his love and mercy? Are you going to write letters of encouragement to those struggling and in need? Are you going to take a pot of soup to your ill neighbor, and while sitting there with him or her, answer the person's questions about Jesus? Are you going to tell them about this hope that you have within you—a hope that will never go away because it rests in the one who "will never leave you nor forsake you" (Hebrews 13:5, ESV) in the midst of the trial?

My friend, you, too, have a voice. Your voice cannot reach the places I can. My voice cannot reach the places yours can. God put you on this earth "for such a time as this" (Esther 4:14, ESV). You have one voice, one life, one chance to be on this earth. What are you going to do?

A stocking-shaped ornament with bent wire, worn beads, and for sale as if new sat in the pristine tree farm's gift shop. I had hoped to find another stocking with the word "hope" on it, but the battered one was the only one left. I did not ask for a price cut and took it home all the same. Later that night, I was lying on my bed, looking at the beaten-up ornament. Suddenly, I realized that was exactly like my hope at that moment. Bruised, beaten up, bent out of shape. What was I doing sitting with the other new and shiny ornaments? I felt out of place and feeling as other people appeared to have it all together on the outside, while my hope was wavering.

I had wanted to leave church and go home that morning. Everyone testified that a sweet Spirit filled the service, one that I, too, subtly felt in a way so tender to me. I cried and cried as our worship band played each song.

What is wrong with me? I am a mess. I should just go home. I thought. But I knew my then boyfriend and I were going to the pumpkin patch after the service, and I just knew I had to hold on until the time of prayer. When the time came for prayer requests, I could hardly speak. But then, the words suddenly flooded and then spewed out of my mouth.

"I had a diagnosis of hyperthyroidism, and I took medicine for it and had one of the typical side effects. Then, my doctor lowered the dose.

Also, I have discovered that the medicine causes me to have head-cold-like symptoms that will not go away. I learned this can be a very severe side effect that happens when your iron levels drop. My only other options for treating hyperthyroidism are a medication that can cause liver damage, radiation, or doing surgery, but I cannot have surgery until the levels go down." I shared during the time of prayer.

I had felt lost and alone going into church, barely able to hold it together. When our pastor began praying, a couple of dear friends met me in the back of the room. They huddled around me, laid hands on me, and began praying. I felt the love and peace of God flow through me for the first time since my diagnosis, and my anxious heart slowly calmed.

When the prayer ended, I could hardly wait to hug each of them. I was slowly regaining my ability to hope. God still has a plan for me, and even if the worst happens, there is still hope, still a purpose. Do you want to know why? Because you, yes you, you get to know my story. You have sat with me during all of these chapters and now you are right here with me, reading these very words I have written during one of the hardest seasons I have faced, and I get to share about the hope that God gave me during this time.

My friend, there is still hope for you. There is still hope when life looks bleak. When you get the diagnosis that you have been dreading to hear. God can use your story, too, to pass along his words of faith, hope, and love. With having God in your life, you are not alone, just like I was not alone. I had my friends who came to my side at church, and I had the Lord right there by my side when things were looking bleak.

And, my friend, I still have hope. A broken hope is still hope when you turn the broken pieces over to the Lord, because he will take them from your outstretched hands and give them life and a purpose. Nothing is better than walking with the Lord and being in his plans for your life.

Looking back now, I can see where the Lord has taken me and am so thankful he walked with me through that difficult time in my life. A year later, I still have the broken ornament as a reminder that even when my hope was broken, God did not leave me alone. I am now doing well on medication and currently taking lower and lower doses. Praise the Lord! God brought me through just like he always does.

If you are going through a rough spot like I was, if you are dealing with something that seems crippling to your faith, if you have stood for as long as you can, I want you to know that I am praying for you. Right now, as I write these words, I am praying for you, that you'll see God's hope and future for you. Jeremiah 29:11 (NIV) says, "'For I know the plans I have for you,' declares the Lord, 'plans to prosper you and not to harm you, plans to give you hope and a future.'"

God sees you, my friend.

He is using your story—and all of those that proclaim his glory—to change the world around us. As in, the world being our neighbor, the people we come into contact with each day—anyone who is brought into our area of the world or the area of the world God brings us to. And the Lord can use your witness to reach others to come into a relationship with him. We need to let him steer our life and tell us where to go and who to tell about him, because if we try to do it ourselves, we will crash.

That little white sock-shaped ornament with the word "hope" shared a little bit of encouragement, reminding me that I am not the only one who has struggled in having hope in the hard times of life. But, the ornament is also a reminder that God can fill me up with his hope, even when I feel discouraged and like hope is impossible. Jesus said in Mark 10:27 (NIV), "With man this is impossible, but not with God; all things are possible with God."

The Lord will help where we are lacking if we will just ask for his help. That ornament I bought is the only one of its kind, perhaps a little beaten up, but loved all the same. Just four letters, H-O-P-E.

Katy Nichole has a profound song called, "God is in this Story." The song tells of how God is in the story of your life. He is in all of the little details and parts that may not have seemed like much at the time, but looking back you can see God's hand over your life. With God, our hope is not gone. We remember that he never failed us before and he will not start failing us now. God is in every detail of your life, weaving it together into a beautiful book, an impactful story that is going to touch the lives of others around you. So, when the storms of life come, turn to Jesus and let your hope rest in him. Jesus did not let you go before and he is not going to start now. He has got you in the palm of his hand. He is working on your story, your testimony, and it is going to help people all around you.[xviii]

Just like you, God is in my story too. He is in all of the torn and tear-stained pages of my book and life. When the storm barrels down, and when I'm at my weakest, I am still going to trust in Jesus on the mountains and in the valleys. At my best and at my worst. At my strongest and my weakest. I am going to trust him. He never fails. He always works it out.

What about you? Is he in your story? Are you going to trust him no matter what? He NEVER fails.

Review Questions

- Is God in your story?
- What situation are you giving to God and leaving in his trust-worthy hands?

Scripture memory verse:

Job 13:15 (ESV)
"Though he slay me, I will hope in him"

Challenge:

Thank the Lord for the Christian mentors and friends he has added to your life. Pray for God to continually place prayer warriors in your life who you can trust to pray with you and for you.

FAITH

HOPE

LOVE

What's Next?

"What's next?" was already answered when you accepted Jesus into your life. From that moment on, the faithful believer has had the Holy Spirit walking by his or her side and showing him or her the path to take and teaching them the knowledge they need to have to be equipped for the battle.

The thought of *What's next?* came to me a year or two after I rededicated my life to Christ. I knew I believed in God, but I did not know how to grow from the baby Christian I was to the level where my mature Christian friends were. They believed no matter what and always knew the right thing to say. All I knew was I had believed in Jesus' name.

The Holy Spirit gave me a word, (faith, hope, love) that we focused on together, and he used those words to teach me more about the Lord and what I was to do next. And I fully believe he will do the same for you if you ask him to teach you what is next for you.

Now, it is your turn to share through your own God-given gifts.

First of all, you can share your faith. You can do this by sharing about the Lord with a friend. If you know the Lord, then you can introduce him to others, too. In a way it is like, "You are my friend, and God is my friend, and I would love it if the two of you got the chance to meet. God this is So-and-so, So-and-so this is my friend God."

My Bible has the plan of salvation written in the back, and it is one of my favorite things about this specific Bible. It first gives a summary of the Christian faith, starting with Genesis and Adam and Eve, and then discusses Jesus and his death on the cross and the redemption that brought the world, why we need to be saved, how we need to be saved, and more. On the very last page it says a prayer and asks if you believe.

"The verse John 11:26 actually ends with Jesus asking, 'Do you believe this?' It is a question that every person must answer. Do you believe that Jesus Christ is the Son of God? Is Jesus the object of your faith? Not faith in ritual, not faith in sacrifices, not faith in morals, not faith in yourself. Do you believe that Jesus died on the cross to free you from the guilt and judgment of sin? Do you believe that He rose from the grave, breaking the power of death and making a way for you to have eternal life in heaven? If so, you may express your faith in Him by praying this prayer,

"Heavenly Father, I believe that Jesus Christ is Your Son, and that He died on the cross to save me from my sin. I believe that He rose again to life, and that He invites me to live forever with Him in heaven as part of Your family. Because of what Jesus has done, I ask You to forgive me of my sin and give me eternal life. I invite You to come into my heart and life. I want to trust Jesus as my Savior and follow him as my Lord. Help me to live in a way that pleases and honors You. Amen."[xix]

We have received the greatest gift from the greatest giver: eternal life. God wants us to be with him forever in Heaven, but he gives us a choice. Will we choose him or chose the world? That same choice is offered to every human on this planet. Will you be the one to share about him? When he says, "Whom will I send?" Will you say, "Send me?" (Isaiah 6:8 NIV) Who will you share the gospel with?

Next, you can share about the hope he has given you to encourage another. Share through a testimony. Or visit someone in the hospital. Or sit with a friend when she is going through a tough time. So many people are lonely on this earth. We have a larger population than ever before, and more people are lonely than ever before. Will you be that much-needed connection? Will you strengthen someone's hope by taking a minute to encourage him or her? You never know what kind of impact you will leave after you are gone.

A few years ago, one of my dear friends passed away in his sleep. I had just seen him a few weeks before this. He was the same as he had always been: friendly, sharing God's love and a wonderful friend to all. He and his wife made beautiful, handmade wooden crosses; each looked identical, but you would have to know what you were looking for to be able to find any differences. The night I heard of his passing, I sat quietly, holding the cross and reflecting on so many memories over the years.

When I first started serving with the Christian organization called the Great Banquet in 2016, this couple was there. I was on the kitchen team with the husband as one of our leaders. He gave each of the ladies on the kitchen team a hand-carved cross. I have carried the cross he gave me in my prayer journal case since that day. His wife recently handed out more of the crosses they made at another Great Banquet weekend just a few weeks before he died. I now have one of their crosses from the first time I met them to the last few weeks he was here on this earth.

This couple encouraged me when I was first helping out with the Banquet and was so nervous about being on one of the teams. They re-minded me that the situation was in God's hands, and I needed to give it to him. They had a kind word and encouragement to share with me each time I saw them. I have treasured calling them friends. Their crosses have quickly become among my most sentimental possessions and are used frequently by many others who received them, too. I was talking with the wife a couple of weeks ago, when she gave me the second cross. My first cross was made out of oak. This one was made out of spalted maple.

"Do you know why it looks like that?" She had asked me. I had never heard of it before and looked at the dark lines running throughout the cross. Then she told me, "The maple has fungus in it. You have to get the wood at just the right time or else it will fall apart." The maple had begun to decay, but it was stopped at the right time, just before crum-bling apart upon handling. The maple had begun to decay, but was now a prized work of art.

We, too, can help stop the decay process in someone by pointing him or her to Jesus. He can pause that nasty decay that likes to spread in us, and instead, the Lord turn us into a beautiful work of art. The decay is no longer our demise but now our testimony. The decay, the sin, the bitterness, the heartache, the despair, the lies can be paused and frozen in place, never to take hold of us again.

The decay happened, but the wood was still usable! Each believer has a testimony of how God intervened in our lives, how God still used us just like that piece of maple has a story embedded into it.

Our lives are like the spalted maple, and when we share our testimony, it is like passing around that cross. Everybody that knows me knows that I did not create it; I have never done any woodworking. Everyone knows that the Creator created the spalted maple in the first place. No one else can place the fungus so perfectly in perfect lines and cause it to happen so profoundly as the Creator.

Everyone who sees the work that was put into making the cross can know that my friends worked at forming the crosses much like Jesus does in restoring our lives. Not one cross was the exact same, all were a little different but you knew what each one was supposed to be, all of them were made into the shape of a cross. All Christians are a little different. We are different colors with different backgrounds, but all of us who believe in and follow him, are Christians. We have been brought out of our past and given a new life. The testimony remains, for with it all may see what God has done for you and me.

Finally, share the love he has given you. Remember Sally and Jenny? Do not selfishly hold on to the love he has given you; instead, share his love, and in doing so keep from turning sour.

I love sour candy, but it is hard to love sour people, much less to be one. My friend always says, "If you are what you eat then I want to be sweet."

I am not suggesting this as a life motto, but to instead say, "If I am what I put in me, all of the shows I watch, the things I listen to, and the people I choose to be around, then am I being the best witness I can be? Or am

I putting in refreshing, spirit-filled friendships, and time spent in prayer and reading my Bible so that I can grow into the best witness I can be?"

I have not always been the best at spending time with God, and when I do not, I feel lousy and my mood can be sour. Sweetness is spending time with God. He is the one who pours out the good stuff onto and through us.

Some ways we can help share the love we have been given are by serving and volunteering. Remember that miracle man I spoke of in Faith: As We Grow? His wife is continuing the kids' club, lovingly named the Hot Dog Club after they shared their first real meal together. On October 4, 2023, Christian musician Danny Gokey visited the Hot Dog Club and renovated my friend's backyard by adding a large back deck, digging a ditch so the backyard would not flood when it rains, and added air conditioning to the food storage shed so they would not lose their food when it was really hot.

Their team also added a sign with my friends on it and the name of the Hot Dog Club. God was working wonders in their lives, and he has continued to do so to this day. God has his hand on the Hot Dog Club, and if God says it stays, then it stays.

There is hope for those kids who attend the Hot Dog Club. They have food and water and people from all over the nation are helping to take care of them by sending support. My friends did not know what God was going to bring from a cup of water on a hot day, but God knew their hearts and planted a fruitful ministry right from the front door of their own home.

God pulls us out of the comfortable into the needed. My friend's house overflowed with food before they had the storage shed. They had to run home many times because someone needed something to eat. We will never know for sure just how many lives a cup of water can impact and how far God will stretch us. But stretching helps us grow.

"Then Moses stretched out his hand over the sea, and all that night the Lord drove the sea back with a strong east wind and turned it into dry land. The waters were divided, and the Israelites went through the

sea on dry ground, with a wall of water on their right and on their left"
(Exodus 14:21–22, NIV).

God asked Moses to *stretch* out his hand over the sea. Moses' faithfulness and trust in God took place before the miracle did. And for countless
years, the Israelites recited this very event and a reminder of God's faithfulness to them. In the stretching, he sees our faithfulness. We might be
stretched in ways we would have never thought possible. But remember,
nothing is impossible with God.

We cannot be ready to share about faith, hope, and love if we have
not first learned of them ourselves. You will find that this book is not the
only way God will be revealing himself to and teaching you. God will
keep showing you more and more about faith, hope, and love through
your reading of his Word, the Bible, and through prayer and situations
he brings your way. Remember that the process is a journey, and we are
always growing in faith, hope, and love.

When I was a young child, my uncle and I were building a wall of
blocks. When we finished the three-fourths of a circle of blocks, I sat inside for a picture. Seconds later, my brother came tearing through the
blocks, and they ended up in a scattered mess on the floor. Like the blocks,
I did not build a strong enough foundation in my life, and when the world
or the evil one tried to tear me down, he succeeded. But the funny thing
about bricks is, after the wall falls apart, the bricks can be stacked again.
Those blocks I was building as a kid were built back up again one day
stronger than before.

The devil hates God. He hates all who follow the Lord. The devil is going to try to make your life as miserable as possible, but you do not have
to let him win. You have no solid foundation if you say that the world is
your foundation. It is like saying quicksand is your foundation. You will
just sink. We can trust in God instead and let him build us up. We can be
like the wise man and build our house on the rock by having Jesus be our
foundation. Let the Lord build on your foundation of Jesus.

Jesus was called the cornerstone. I once heard that the cornerstone set the build for the entire structure. If they did not have a good cornerstone, the building would not stand firm. It was an important part of any building back in Biblical days. Let Jesus be your cornerstone and set the build for the rest of your life.

Why is it so important to share all of this with other people? Why do we need to share about love, hope, and faith? Well, I will tell you this. One day, a young girl thought her life was over. She laid down ready to go on to the next life. If that girl had succeeded, she would have likely never met any of the people in this book. She would have never learned that there is more to life. She would have never known that she could have Christian friends. She would have never known God's love for her. She would have never known her calling. She would have never known her God given name. She would have never met the love of her life. She would have never met her nephews. She would have never come back to live at the camp she grew up attending with her grandparents. She would have never met anyone who would become some of her dearest friends. She would have never known God's love for the redeemed. She would have never known there was hope for her. She would have never known that she could have faith in God.

Two days later, her life had changed forever. And she would have never known that she was not the last to feel that way too.

Because of Jesus, she could know that her life had a purpose. Because of Jesus, she knew that he had a plan for her. Because of Jesus, she was redeemed. Because of Jesus turning her life around, she could help others do so, too. Because of Jesus, she got to lead others to Jesus. Because of Jesus, she knew that she was not done living yet. Because of Jesus, she got to share about God's faithfulness on the other side of the world. Because of Jesus, she had a new life. Because of Jesus, she met people who would mentor her in the Christian faith. Because of Jesus, she would survive that day and many other days. Because of Jesus, she has a family that loves her. Because of Jesus, she has godly friends. Because of Jesus, she has hope. Because of Jesus, she has faith. Because of Jesus, she is loved and can love. Because of Jesus, she is me, and I am going to walk this journey with God. He has never failed me.

Because Jesus gave me a new life, I was able to meet a woman who became dear to my heart. She lived in a nursing home down the street from my college. I had just rededicated my life to Christ, and I had begun visiting the nursing home on Sundays for their 2 p.m. church service. When I saw her, she was quiet and sitting alone in a wheelchair.

During the songs, she sat there silently with her book turned to the wrong page. My heart was burdened for her, and I asked if I could sit with her. I sat down beside her and helped her turn the pages to the correct songs and sang along with the rest of the crowd. Slowly, she began softly singing along with me. We listened to the message and then church was dismissed.

After the service she told me her name, Marcelene. She could barely see or hear me talking to her. I was so moved that she came to the church services even though she probably could not hear most of it. After service, the residents needed help back to their rooms, and I took Marcelene to hers. After we got there, we sat and talked and talked. This was in 2012, and in that time period of my life, I had recently rededicated my life to Christ and was learning about having Christian friendships. I felt very lonely. This woman became a friend of mine.

Almost every Sunday, I attended the service and then sat with Marcelene afterwards in her room. She told me about her son who lived nearby and would come to visit her, and I told her about what I was going through in life at that time. I was like a baby Christian and everything seemed *big*. Big feelings, big hurts, big fears. I was dealing with it all, even after rededicating my life to Christ. I had a new life but God had to change my old way of thinking and help me see things the way He saw them.

One day, I invited the dorm's chaplain to come with me to the nursing home. She was the sweetest person and quickly became my friend too. I was so excited to have someone at school that wanted to spend time with me. During one of our first days visiting the nursing home together, my friend and I walked through each of the rooms, stopping to talk with anyone that was alert and wanted a visitor.

We met an author and pianist who was an incredible woman with an amazing life story. *Wow! An author! She did it! She actually wrote a book many years ago! I wonder if I will ever publish someday?* I had asked myself. Amazingly, you are holding the answer to that very question today.

As we walked towards Marcelene's room, we stopped to visit a woman across the hall from her. My college friend found out that Marcelene's neighbor was well known at the school we attended. The woman had been very involved throughout her lifetime, and later on I learned of friends of hers. My college friend and I each found someone who had made an impression on us, and we both made a friend at the nursing home.

Sundays my college friend and I would meet and then walk to the nursing home's church service together. After service, we would visit with our friends and walk back to the school again.

I visited with Marcelene for a year. I know I was able to be a blessing to her, as well as she was for me. After a few months of visiting with each other, I could tell she was truly happy to see me, and she always welcomed me in. One year for Christmas I made her a card with puffballs and pipe cleaners so she could "see" it. She was asleep when I got to her room, but by the next Sunday the card had been moved to display atop her dresser, and I hoped she was able to read it. Time seemed to stand still or perhaps it continued on repeat as I looked forward to our Sunday visits week after week.

At the end of the school year, I told her it was time for me to go back to Illinois, and I would not be there for a while. For the first time in my life I said, "I'll see you again soon" instead of "goodbye." I started to say goodbye, but for some reason I never did. That was the last time I saw Marcelene.

You see, after I accepted the Lord in my life, I was not passionate about my major and switched careers. God was shifting my heart into His plans, which were so much better than my own. I had taken general education classes for a semester, and my parents and I realized that I could not continue going to the university I was attending, as college was not cheap.

That October, I went to China instead of returning to the university. Almost five years passed before I was able to go to visit Marcelene again. I walked straight to her room and stood at the door. New names I did not know were at that door that day. I asked the nurses at the desk if they knew of her, and they did not. Sullenly I walked back outside to where my grandparents were waiting for me. "Were you able to find her?"

I sadly shook my head "no." Marcelene was gone, and I never even said got to say goodbye.

Almost ten years after I had told Marcelene, "I'll see you again soon." I found out that Marcelene had died on September 8, 2014 at the nursing home where I had gone to so many times to visit with her. I was crushed. I had waited too long.

Do not wait until it is too late to share God's love, the hope that you have, and your faith with someone. I was too late to tell Marcelene goodbye. I was too late to give her one more hug or to have one more of her grandmotherly kisses on the cheek. It is too late, and I cannot go back.

I know I will see Marcelene in Heaven someday, and I look forward to wrapping my arms around her in the biggest hug ever. Marcelene was my first Christian friend after I rededicated my life to Christ. But if there is one statement I can tell you from this experience, it would be: *Do not wait until it is too late.*

You may think there will be another day, but if God says *today,* then go today. You may not get tomorrow to do it over again. Take advantage of the opportunities he has given you today. Do not let them pass you like I did with seeing Marcelene one last time. God can still give us another chance, but we do not always get a second, third, fourth chance.

One day the Lord showed me that Marcelene was a Christian. And as a Christian, it is not "Goodbye," but it really is "I will see you again soon."

I believe that Marcelene made it into Heaven and I look forward to reconnecting with her when I get there. And, I can wrap my arms around her neck and tell her how much I have loved her and how much she meant to me. And, if she had a view into my life at all, or if the Lord passed on the message, I look forward to her knowing how far I have come with God from that little, scared, worried, bitter believer I was at the beginning into a believer who really loves God for who he is.

God has done a mighty work in me, and this book only tells the beginning. God will grow you into the strong, mature believer; it just takes time. And he is good at time. He is good at building a strong foundation and giving us the right building blocks to make us strong in him. God knows what you need and when you need it. He sends the Holy Spirit to the believer to guide us on our path.

Jesus is our foundation, and he is going to be right there with us. The Lord is all we need to build ourselves on a Christ-Centered foundation, and he is going to help you along the way, as you trust in him. God bless you my brothers and sisters in Christ.

God loves you. So, what are you going to do about it? Are you going to love him back deeper than ever before? Are you going to proclaim his name from the mountains or even in your workplace? Are you going to stand firm on your faith and share it with your neighbor? Are you going to live for Christ every step of the way? Are you going to hold onto your hope until your last day, when your faith shall become sight? Are you going to go to your Marcelenes, your Peters, your Marys, your Sallys or your Jennys? Are you going to answer the Lord's call: *Whom shall I send?*

Is your answer *Send me?*

Ecclesiastes 12:13 (NASB), "The conclusion, when everything has been heard, is: fear God and keep His commandments, because this applies to every person."

Notes:

i   Catherine Soanes and Angus Stevenson, eds., *Concise Oxford English Dictionary* (Oxford: Oxford University Press, 2004).

ii   Pastor Mike. "As believers, We are all just walking each other Home." A Heart for God Ministries. n.p., 19 Mar. 2019. Web. 23 July 2022.

iii West, Matthew. "Do Something." Track 4 on *Into the Light*. Sparrow Records, 2012.

iv Morgan, Robert. *Then Sings My Soul*, (Nashville: Thomas Nelson, Inc, 2002), 276-277.

v   Carson, D. *NIV Zondervan Study Bible*, (Grand Rapids, MI: Zondervan, 2015) 2014.

vi   Carson, D. *NIV Zondervan Study Bible*, (Grand Rapids, MI: Zondervan, 2015), 2182.

vii Bolinger, Hope. "Why Is John the "Disciple Whom Jesus Loved"?" *Bible Study Tools*, 16 Dec. 2022, www.biblestudytools.com/bible-study/topical-studies/why-is-john-the-disciple-whom-jesus-loved.html. Accessed 27 Jan. 2023.

viii Got Questions Ministries, *Got Questions? Bible Questions Answered* (Bellingham, WA: Logos Bible Software, 2002–2013).

ix   Grant, John. "Justice, Mercy, and Grace." The Life, 5 July 2015. https://thelife.com/devotionals/justice-mercy-and-grace.

x   *Amplified Bible* (AMP) (La Habra, CA: The Lockman Foundation, 2015).

xi   n.d. "Quick Search Commandment." *Bible Gateway*. Accessed 22 February, 2023. https://www.biblegateway.com/quicksearch/?quicksearch=commandment&version=ESV.

xii *Holy Bible, New Living Translation*, (Carol Stream, IL: Tyndale House Publishers, Inc, 1996, 2004, 2015)

xiii Bates, Noel. "Sermon at Frankfort Camp Ministries." 9 July 2019.

xiv Carson, D. *NIV Zondervan Study Bible*, (Grand Rapids, MI: Zondervan, 2015), 2685.

xv   Carson, D. *NIV Zondervan Study Bible*, (Grand Rapids, MI: Zondervan, 2015), 454-455.

xvi Carson, D. *NIV Zondervan Study Bible*. (Grand Rapids, MI: Zondervan, 2015). 2545-2546

xvii Big Daddy Weave 'Redeemed.' AZLyrics.com, Accessed June 4, 2023. https://www.azlyrics.com/lyrics/bigdaddyweave/redeemed.html

xviii Nichole, Katy "God is in This Story." AZLyrics.com, Accessed February 23, 2024. https://www.azlyrics.com/lyrics/katynichole/godisinthisstory.html

xix *The Holy Bible, English Standard Version*. ESV® (Wheaton, IL: Crossway. a publishing ministry of Good News Publishers, 2011), 1045.

www.ingramcontent.com/pod-product-compliance
Lightning Source LLC
Chambersburg PA
CBHW071220090426
42736CB00014B/2909